BEYOND THE MORTAL COIL

An exploration of life, death and all that exists in-between

By

PATRICIA SUTCLIFFE

(best selling author)

COPYRIGHT © 2025 PATRICIA SUTCLIFFE

ALL RIGHTS RESERVED

IBNS:9798298873918

THE MORAL RIGHT OF THE AUTHOR HAS BEEN ASSERTED

NAMES HAVE BEEN CHANGED TO PROTECT THE ANONYMITY OF PARTICIPANTS OTHER THAN WHERE PERMISSION TO USE ACTUAL NAMES WERE GIVEN

DEDICATION

This book is dedicated to all of those whose paranormal experiences are dismissed or ridiculed.

And

To those who have supported me and encouraged me to continue through all adversities.

ACKNOWLEDGMENTS

To my beta readers, Adam and Alice

To Paul Cooper for my front cover design

To John and Phyllis, Alice, Edwin and all the others who told me their stories. You have my appreciation.

CONTENTS

1. Introduction
2. The Amazing World of Psychic Phenomena

    Historical Revelations and Belief

    Sceptics versus Believers: A Healthy Debate

    The Gap Between Science and Spirituality

3. The Fabric of Consciousness and Reality
4. A Glimpse of the Other Side (NDEs)
5. Do Guardian Angels Guide Us?
6. Multiple Lives, Multiple Journeys
7. Out of Body Freedoms (OBEs)
8. Sixth Sense Verses Mystical Trickery
9. Ghosts and All Things Scary
10. The Future of Psychic Phenomena
11. Conclusion
12. About the Author

Beyond The Mortal Coil

1. Introduction:

Have you ever wondered what lies beyond our human existence or asked yourself, 'What is beyond the everyday reality we know?'

Are you genuinely curious about unseen forces that may influence our lives and the Universe? Have you encountered something 'weird' that has occurred to you? Something you cannot explain, something you can only describe as supernatural, that makes you feel there is more beyond what you know.

Life, with its joys and sorrows, is undoubtedly a profound and mysterious journey, but does it all end with death? Or is there something that transcends our earthly demise and goes beyond what we know and accept? Something beyond the realm of scientific understanding, which forms the basis of much of our reality.

Why do we have such a profound interest in the Universe and the anomalies that shape our existence and prompt us to question our reality? What causes so many to believe in the afterlife, and why do many rational individuals discuss metaphysical experiences and supernatural phenomena? People throughout history and from all corners of the globe, young and old. How much longer can we continue to dismiss the possibility that there is something beyond our comprehension? A realm that might exist, surpassing the limits of reason and logic.

In 'Beyond the Mortal Coil', I invite both the curious and the sceptical to explore life's mysteries with me and embark on a journey into the world of the unknown. The fascinating world of metaphysics and the unexplainable that shadows our very existence.

We will examine the mystical experiences reported by individuals from various backgrounds, including children, scientists, and academics. My first unexplained experience happened when I was eleven years old. It left me bewildered and questioning my senses. We will explore that, and many more occurrences experienced by others and myself as we journey into the unknown.

Events such as near-death experiences (NDEs) offer those who have undergone them profound insights into the other side and the significance of our earthly lives. These experiences have deeply altered their thoughts and beliefs about the afterlife. Should we dismiss the thousands of anecdotes due to scepticism, or is it time to consider the possibility of an existence beyond what we currently know and understand?

Out-of-body experiences (OBEs) occur when comatose patients can recall events and conversations that transcend human understanding. We will explore the fascinating realm of psychic phenomena and paranormal events, which are an undeniable reality to those who experience them.

Does our consciousness move on beyond the material body? We have explored this question throughout time, and scientists who find no logical answer to the dilemma still consider it a 'hard question'. What is the link between consciousness and how we perceive our reality? Will we ever know?

Do we have "Guardian Angels," or are they merely myths created to connect the material world with the spiritual? Are we truly guided, or do we navigate our life paths on our own? What role does faith play in our personal beliefs about the existence of an afterlife? To what extent are we influenced and shaped by religion?

What do we mean when discussing having a 'Sixth Sense', and what is this? The phrase 'trust your intuition' is a common one we often hear. Could this be what is meant by our sixth sense, seen as the opening of the Pineal Gland by many?

Is it possible that we reincarnate, journeying through time and space? Many religions, including Buddhism, Sikhism, and Hinduism, embed the belief in reincarnation into their teachings. Regression into past lives has also become a feature in many meditation practices, with hypnotherapy gaining ground to enable the curious to travel back into the past. Can it be that our souls have multiple life experiences?

What about the historical perspectives? In religious and philosophical texts, we find the belief in the afterlife. In ancient Greek mythology, we also find accounts of near-death experiences. In 'The Republic,' Plato tells the story of Er, who returns from the afterlife to recount his experiences. Er was a soldier who had died in battle returned to reveal how our souls are judged on the deeds of our past lives. Plato used this to reinforce the nature of justice. Recounting life's actions through playbacks is a common theme in modern-day NDEs.

The debate between science and spirituality has been extensively discussed, with the central difference being one of proof and belief. Are we saying that if we cannot prove something using the scientific method, it cannot exist? Or is it time that science and metaphysical phenomena learned to coexist?

"Beyond the Mortal Coil" invites you to take a deeper look into the mysteries of life and what may come after. It's all about exploring psychic phenomena and the afterlife through both personal stories and the experiences of others. My goal is to inspire a shift in how we approach these topics, which are often overlooked and under-appreciated.

As I reflect on this journey, I'm reminded of an old Chinese saying: "The best time to plant a tree was twenty years ago. The second-best time is now." This resonates deeply, reminding us that the quest for understanding remains timeless and enduring. Just as a tree needs time and nurturing to grow strong, our understanding of life and the afterlife can also develop if we're open to exploring these ideas.

In "Beyond the Mortal Coil," I aim to spark conversations that transcend conventional beliefs and encourage us to embrace the uncertainty of life. Each chapter challenges you to reflect on your views and fosters curiosity about what makes us human, as well as the possibilities that lie beyond what we can see. Let's uncover new layers of our reality together!

> **A closed mind is like a closed book.
> It's nothing more than a block of wood.**
>
> Anon

2. The Amazing World of Psychic Phenomena

When I embarked upon my journey to author this book, I expected to be met with scepticism and disdain. I was wrong. Instead, family, friends and strangers rushed forward to tell me of the unexplained things they had experienced, adding to the many psychic phenomena that abound on media platforms and books alike.

Paula, a long-standing acquaintance of sound mind and body, told me the following account:

'I was only a young kid when my dad got a new job, and we moved to a new house. It smelled fusty, and I wasn't comfortable being there. I wanted to be back with my friends. The only good part was that I had a bedroom to myself instead of sharing one with my older sister, Sal. Anyway, one night, I woke up with someone pulling my bedclothes off me. I thought it was Sal messing about.

I sat up and could sense someone looking at me, but I couldn't see anyone. Then I felt something touch my leg. I was scared but calm at the same time. I seemed to know it wasn't trying to hurt me but wanted me to know it was there. I shouted, 'Go away, you're scaring me.' It at once disappeared. I got up and ran downstairs. My mother told me I was having nightmares and kicking my bedding off myself.

It never happened again, but we discovered that my room was where an old lady had died. She was the owner's mother who sold the house to my parents. It scared me then, but now I think she was checking who was in her room.'

Like many others, Paula stressed that nothing would convince her that it had not happened. I understood her need to emphasise that her experience was real. I assured her I didn't doubt her story, and I explained to her the strange occurrences I had experienced.

I vividly remember the details of my first experience at eleven years old, and, like Paula, nothing will convince me it wasn't real.

I had left my mother and sister singing the song 'Sailor' by Petula Clark. They were in the downstairs living room as I went upstairs to bed. It was late, and I was tired. I was also envious of the closeness they shared. I drifted off to sleep, only to wake later to hear them still singing the same song. Their voices were crystal clear. I sat up and stared, alarmed, because I had listened to my sister come to bed, and I knew she was asleep across the room. Confused, I walked up the corridor to my parents' bedroom to see my mother sleeping. Yet, I could hear them singing with absolute clarity.

Returning to my bed, I found it difficult to go back to sleep. I knew I wasn't mad; the song was being sung clearly. I couldn't explain it then, and I cannot explain it now, but I know it happened. The next day, I told my mother about my experience. She dismissed it as a dream. My sister was more than a little bemused and mocked my sanity. My protestations of walking up the corridor fell on deaf ears, and I put it to one side, but I never forgot that night.

Years later, while studying psychology, I encountered an American psychologist and writer, Ulric Neisser (Cognitive Psychology,) (1967), who coined the term "echoic memory." He described a type of memory related to the brief and temporary storage of auditory sounds that leaves a trace in your echoic memory but lasts only a short time.

It was then that I vividly remembered the song 'Sailor' that replayed in my echoic memory. Or did I experience a psychic event? You decide. I don't know the answer.

Regardless of our thoughts on mystical events, we cannot deny their reality to those who have had such experiences, which often change their beliefs and how they choose to lead their lives as a result. This is especially true of NDEs. So, what exactly are we discussing when examining metaphysical occurrences and the extensive research conducted in areas such as spirituality, the paranormal, NDEs, mysticism, and other enigmatic phenomena that traditional scientific methods cannot explain? Researchers study metaphysical experiences better to understand questions about reality, consciousness, and existence. These experiences go beyond what science can easily explain.

People have always wondered about the unknown and searched for meaning in life. Many want to find their purpose and understand if there's more to life than meets the eye. Some turn to religion or meditation to feel more connected to something greater, while others look for answers in science and psychology.

Interest in the afterlife, other dimensions, and ideas like near-death experiences (NDEs) is widespread. Many who have had an NDE claim to have visited other realms, but these stories are deeply personal and open to interpretation. It's essential to keep an open mind, even if we can't prove everything scientifically.

Belief in supernatural and higher powers existed long before modern science. Ancient cultures, such as Native American tribes and the Aztecs, held their own beliefs about the afterlife and the destiny of souls, which were influenced by traditions and social status.

Science now tries to explore these mysteries, with research in quantum physics and neuroscience looking into consciousness and what might happen beyond physical life.

Why are people so fascinated with the afterlife and mystical experiences? As we age and face our mortality, we often look for comfort in the idea that something greater exists beyond death. Whether or not this is true, there is a lot of information and personal accounts suggesting there may be more than our physical world.

When exploring metaphysical experiences, it's helpful to consider cultural and religious influences, both from the past and present.

For example, the Dalai Lama writes in the Tibetan Book of the Dead that many ancient schools of thought believed in a soul or consciousness that exists independently from the body and mind. Today, people talk about the soul and consciousness as similar concepts, and online communities discuss these topics openly.

Some people will always reject new ideas out of fear or habit, but others will be eager to explore the unknown and learn from these experiences.

Not that belief in the afterlife and the occurrence of metaphysical experience is the same for everyone. The scope and level change drastically from person to person, community to community, and country to country. Much of this depends upon religious teachings and internalised feelings about life.

Some question the authenticity of mediums and clairvoyants, suggesting they prey on the gullibility of desperate people. At the same time, others see reincarnation and the afterlife as natural processes governed by spiritual laws, just as rules govern our physical world.

When we examine the rules governing the spiritual realm, the Law of Karma comes to mind immediately. It is widely understood that our actions will influence future events through the cause-and-effect rule. What you sow, you will reap.

We are also very familiar with the Law of Attraction and our understanding that our thoughts, whether negative or positive, significantly impact our life experiences and the energy we emit. Negative energy attracts bad luck, while positive energy brings good luck.

The law of Oneness is now coming to the fore increasingly with the belief that we are all interconnected by a much greater whole and that we are one with the Universe.

Those who have had an NDE will speak of the Law of Love, explaining that they felt tremendous love during their experience. Some relate this to an immediate knowing that love is what we must strive to live by on Earth, and that only that will lead us to actual spiritual growth.

While interpreting these laws remains subjective and dependent on belief systems, religion, and culture, we cannot fail to see people applying them to their lives in search of spiritual fulfilment.

My goal is not to convince you of any particular viewpoint; I aim to spark your curiosity and encourage you to embark on the journey. It promises to be one of revelation and self-discovery. Who knows, you may find yourself transformed by the insights you gain.

Historical Revelations and Beliefs

Belief in the afterlife and paranormal experiences isn't new; in fact, people have talked about these ideas for thousands of years. Ancient Greek philosopher Plato, for example, believed that the world we see is just a shadow of a perfect, invisible world. In his writing "Phaedo," he argued that the soul lives on after the body dies. He also thought that our senses can't grasp what happens after death, and that the human soul is just passing through this world, using the body as a temporary home.

The Ancient Egyptians also held a strong belief in an afterlife. This is evidenced by the tombs uncovered by archaeologists, which were filled with belongings intended to assist the deceased in the next world. The Egyptian "Book of the Dead" (written between approximately 1550 and 1070 BC) served as a guide for souls to navigate the afterlife and face judgment based on their actions in life, ideas that still appear in modern stories of near-death experiences.

Not all ancient cultures saw the afterlife as a happy place. The Mesopotamians, for instance, imagined a shadowy, gloomy existence after death. The famous poem "The Epic of Gilgamesh" tells the story of a man's search for immortality, which teaches that death can't be avoided, but also shows how humans have always wondered about what comes after.

The Mayans, who lived in what is now Mexico and Central America, believed in three worlds: the underworld (Xibalba), the middle world (Earth), and the upper world. They thought that how you lived affected what happened to your soul. Good actions could send you to the upper world, while bad ones could send you to the underworld—an idea like karma found in many religions.

Ancient Chinese culture is also rich in spiritual beliefs and ancestor worship, which remain essential today. It's common to see altars in homes where families honour their ancestors with offerings and seek their guidance. Temples honouring the dead are found throughout China and other parts of Asia. When Buddhism spread in the region, beliefs in reincarnation and karma became part of everyday life. Festivals like the Hungry Ghost Festival, held in places like Singapore, involve giving offerings to keep away evil spirits.

Funeral customs in China are often very elaborate, with rituals designed to bring luck and good health to the living and to help guide the dead into the afterlife. Many believe that the spirits of ancestors are involved in everyday life.

The Tibetan Book of the Dead is a well-known Buddhist text that offers guidance for the dying. Written as early as the 4th century, it's often read to people who are near death to help them prepare for what comes next. It was first published in the West in 1927 and is still read today, as many feel it contains wisdom for the modern world.

No matter the culture, preparing for death often involves living a spiritual life. Practices like meditation help individuals focus on their spiritual journey and release fears about death. Both Eastern and Western traditions continue to incorporate meditation and other methods as part of their quest for meaning and connection with something greater than themselves.

They authored The Tibetan Book of the Dead as a series of teachings, using mantras and verses to explain each phase a person must undergo to liberate their soul as it transcends to the afterlife.

While many ritualist cultures originate from Eastern beliefs and have a long history, they are not the only cultures that believe in the afterlife and metaphysical phenomena. Many Native American tribes honour the spirits of their ancestors and regard their burial grounds as sacred.

Living in harmony with both the living and the dead is essential to their belief. This is accomplished through prayer and meditation, often guided by spiritual teachers. Dancing and shamanic ceremonies are common practices for communicating with the spirit world.

Age-old stories of happy hunting grounds and closeness to nature abound in these tales, which are told around campfires by Indian warriors and chiefs. Many of these tales have their origins in deep-rooted supernatural beliefs. Tribes such as the Navajo, Hopi, Ute, and Pueblo tribes of New Mexico all practice elaborate rituals to communicate with the spirits of the dead, believing that supernatural entities have connections to the natural world.

Some Indian tribes, such as the Adivasi, Nagas, Gond, and Santhal, have deities and gods to whom they pay homage to seek protection and guidance. Music and dance, like those of the American Indian Tribes, play a significant role in their spiritual practices.

What insights do we gain from examining ancient beliefs across various cultures? Whilst they differ from group to group, there are some common themes, and as humans, we need to understand the mysteries of the Universe and what happens to us after we die.

Other themes include preparing the body for its journey to the afterlife. We observe this in burial practices worldwide, particularly in Egypt's mummification tradition. We learn of multiple realms that souls go to. There is a part concerned with moral judgements and the Karmic cause-and-effect principle, but humankind's strong desire for continued existence after death is the pinnacle of all.

Believers' vs Sceptics—A Healthy Debate

Sceptics constantly dismiss metaphysical experiences as subjective accounts given by those who long to believe in the reality of the supernatural. Words such as illusory, superstitious, hallucinations brought on by drugs, or the brain trying to find meanings to unexplained events. These descriptions are commonplace among the scientific community and other non-believers in the paranormal, who are often preoccupied with the lack of scientific explanations. They frequently dismiss such accounts as false beliefs.

In the early twentieth century, it wasn't uncommon to place people with particular views in mental institutions, seen as being delusional, those who heard voices, for example, or reported seeing things not of this Earth.

Believers in supernatural experiences often say these moments changed their lives. They use words like "special," "spiritual," "healing," and "eye-opening" to describe what happened to them. Many feel these experiences connect them to a higher power or something greater than everyday life.

Those who are unsure use a different vocabulary to explain their experiences. Commonly, they refer to them as mysterious, intriguing, ambiguous, strange, and uncanny. Still, they reflect on what it means to them and admit to becoming more curious and open-minded about the possibility of something beyond what they knew.

Alas, it is not so simple; many factors affect our belief in or against the supernatural. There is a significant interaction among psychological, cultural, and individual elements. The way we think is an example. Some of us lean naturally towards intuitive thinking, whilst others are prone to relying on facts and evidence-based information.

Some people only trust things that are proven by science, and they often see supernatural stories as unreliable. This makes them sceptical. Scientists try to explain unusual experiences by finding logical reasons for them, believing there must be a natural cause. Because of this, they may not accept anything that can't be tested or proven.

Cultural and religious diversity make defining cohesion difficult, as both greatly influence beliefs about the afterlife and supernatural events.

An important question is: would most religions exist without the idea of an afterlife? Many faiths teach that being good and moral leads to a connection with the afterlife. If science proved there was no afterlife, it could change what religion means to people.

Our beliefs start forming from birth. They come from our families, cultures, and religions, often before we even know it's happening. Personal experiences can shape beliefs later in life.

Think about your childhood. Parents and guardians pass down their beliefs, which they learned the same way. These early lessons can include ideas that aren't true, but because we learn them so young, we usually don't question them unless something happens to make us think differently.

Culture and society also affect what we believe. For example, a child brought up in a strict religious environment may easily accept the idea of an afterlife and see supernatural events as normal. In contrast, a child raised to question things may become more sceptical.

We seek information that confirms our teachings because it helps us align with our culture and accept group norms and beliefs. The need to belong, therefore, can hinder a curious mind. The pursuit of personal growth and self-improvement may not emerge until we reach our later years. Only then will the individual be more open-minded to new ideas.

Denial and the need for affirmations can burden someone living in an environment of scepticism. One account I received, which pinpointed the depth this can reach, was about a man whom I'll call Robert, who had lived with a scientist for twenty-two years. The scientist dismissed all suggestions of the paranormal and an afterlife as rubbish and unproven. The effect of this on Robert, who was open to spiritual ideas, was that he read such accounts and developed his understanding in secret. The irony is that several of his family members were mediums and firmly believed in the afterlife.

We can see then how cultural beliefs and conditioning can lead us to become sceptics or believers. The gap between the two is closing as more individuals share their own experiences. More books about the metaphysical and the afterlife fill our bookshop shelves and overflow on social media platforms.

Living in a sceptical environment can make affirmations challenging. For example, Robert, a writer, secretly explored spiritual topics since his scientist companion dismissed anything paranormal or related to the afterlife as unproven, even though several of Robert's relatives were mediums. This illustrates how cultural conditioning influences our beliefs. Recently, more people are sharing metaphysical experiences, with books and posts on the afterlife becoming increasingly widespread.

So, we ask ourselves, what can change the ardent sceptic into a believer? The primary factor is that they experience the metaphysical for themselves, which has often been the case.

Eben Alexander, a neurosurgeon once sceptical of the afterlife, changed his views after a week-long coma caused by bacterial meningitis. Despite doctors fearing severe brain damage, he awoke lucid and recounted a near-death experience (NDE) that contradicted scientific explanations. In Proof of Heaven (2012), Alexander describes moving from darkness to a vivid, loving realm where he sensed a consciousness beyond the brain, prompting him to question conventional science.

Alexander describes seeing millions of butterflies, which he knew represented the souls of those who had passed. The fact that we all play a part in the universe's tapestry and are connected spiritually contradicts scientific theories that view the material world as the sole reality, ultimately leading to a sense of mortality.

Because of his NDE, Eben Alexander strongly felt he had received a solid message to share the importance of love, interconnectedness and acceptance of an afterlife with others. He now travels the World and engages in podcasts as an inspirational speaker.

Unsurprisingly, Alexander's account received mixed responses from the medical and scientific community. Some were critical, returning to personal experience without providing a proof argument. Others suggested that his brain may have had some activity, which brought about such experiences, but that this activity might not be detectable through standard methods.

The lack of controlled experiments and peer review caused some to reject Alexander's account. Others were more open to alternative answers and acknowledged that NDEs were very complex and may not be fully explainable. This suggests that the current scientific understanding may be insufficient and that further research is necessary in the field of NDEs.

Not all experiences involved NDEs in the Hodgson family and the Enfield Poltergeist case, which caused some sceptics to rethink their beliefs. This case happened in the late 1970s in a suburb of North London, England. In a highly controversial and widely reported case, the two Hodgson daughters, Janet and her younger sister Margaret, were at the centre of paranormal activity in their home.

Police and investigators reported flying furniture, eerie noises, and voices in the house, later inspiring 'The Conjuring 2'. The possession of eleven-year-old Janet Hodgson, who supposedly levitated and spoke different languages, drew global media attention and led to a thorough inquiry by Maurice Gosse and Guy Lyon Playfair. While some sceptics reconsidered after reviewing the case, others questioned its authenticity, especially since Janet admitted to faking some incidents, whether it was an elaborate hoax or genuine remains unresolved.

The New York Times (July 2016) published an article about the renowned author Sir Arthur Conan Doyle, who created the iconic character Sherlock Holmes. Conan Doyle was a trained doctor and a sceptic of the paranormal for most of his life. However, by the end of his life in 1930, he was an ardent believer. So, what changed his opinions so dramatically that he became an outspoken advocate for spiritualism?

Some say it was in response to the death of his son, Kingsley, during WW1, followed by the deaths of several other family members. Others argue that his interest in spiritualism started with reading a book by the American judge and psychic researcher John Worth Edmonds in 1893. Irrespective of the timing or reasons behind his change of belief, he joined the Society for Psychical Research and founded the 'Ghost Club', of which Charles Dickens and W. B. Yeats were members. Conan Doyle solidified his confidence in spiritualism by authoring twenty books on the subject, in which he emphasised the possibility of communicating with the dead.

Another well-known Victorian poet, Elizabeth Barrett Browning, also went from being a sceptic to a believer after taking part in seances and thinking she had made contact with the dead. Seances were common in the Victorian era, so it wasn't strange for people to attend them. Her husband and some friends were interested in spiritualism, too. Her poetry shows she believed that love and life might continue after death. In her well-known poem Sonnet 43, she talks about her love being so deep that, if God allows it, she'll keep loving even after she dies: "I love thee with the breath, smiles, tears of all my life and, if God chooses, I shall but love thee better after death."

Many factors change a person's beliefs. Typical are those who have undergone NDEs or had OBEs, but less familiar are the accounts and dramatic changes of individuals such as Louis Whitley Strieber. An American horror writer, he is best known for his novels "The Hunger" and "Wolfen." He also wrote a non-fiction book called 'Communion ', which discusses his experiences with what he terms as non-human entities. Published in 1987, it is the story of his encounters with aliens. In his introduction, he states that the book tells the story of one man's attempt to cope with a shattering assault from the unknown. The power of his story is told in the film 'The Mosquito Coast' starring Harrison Ford.

He describes the 'Grays,' as non-human beings, as having taken him aboard a strange craft, where he lost track of time and was examined. He says he communicated with them through telepathy. The US Government has noted many reports of UFO sightings and abductions, and although they have found no solid proof, they acknowledge that there are hundreds of unexplained cases.

Sceptics argue that without solid scientific evidence, claims of alien visits lack credibility and are often explained as hoaxes, misidentifications, or psychological phenomena. Given varied experiences, forming a clear conclusion is difficult; keeping an open mind remains essential when evaluating such reports.

The Gulf Between Science and Spirituality

Many people feel they can't believe in something unless science proves it exists. This makes us doubt personal stories about strange experiences unless they are backed by solid evidence. But does everything have to be tested by science to be real? Some things, like emotions or spiritual moments, are hard to measure and may be beyond what science can explain.

Science is excellent for studying things we can see and test, but it can't easily measure feelings, consciousness, or metaphysical experiences. Most scientists say consciousness is just a product of the brain and stops when the brain stops working. Yet there are reports of people having experiences when their brains are supposedly "dead," raising questions science can't easily answer.

Spiritual beliefs about what happens after death vary widely because of culture and religion. These ideas have been around for centuries, long before modern science. Even though there's no solid scientific proof, many people still believe consciousness might exist beyond the body.

While we can't know for sure if there's an afterlife or if consciousness continues, personal stories suggest it's possible. Metaphysical experiences are tricky for scientists since they don't follow the rules of routine testing. This uncertainty means we should keep an open mind and not dismiss things just because they are hard to measure.

In the last two centuries, more people have shared experiences they can't easily explain, things that seem to go beyond our usual understanding of the world. One reason might be that today people are more open to challenging their own beliefs and less afraid of being doubted or laughed at. Even professionals like doctors and scientists are starting to talk about their own unusual experiences and are willing to explore possibilities outside traditional science.

Science is great at helping us learn about things we can see, measure, or test. It's how we make discoveries and solve problems. But that doesn't mean other approaches, like philosophy or personal stories, aren't valuable. Researchers are now using different methods, including interviews and personal accounts, to study things like near-death experiences.

As humans, we've always wanted to understand who we are and why we're here. That search for meaning continues, whether we look for answers in science, spirituality, or both. The conversation between believers in science and those interested in spiritual ideas is still ongoing—and sometimes heated. However, it seems the gap between the two sides is shrinking, thanks to more critical thinking and a willingness to consider new ideas.

3. The Fabric of Consciousness and Reality

I sit and wonder, aware that my thoughts spin in perpetual motion. I contemplate the miracle of the mind. A gift that can transport us back to the past in a flash, bring us into the present in a single breath or jolt us into the future in an instant. Whisk us off to our first day at school. Place us in our favourite restaurant or holiday retreat. Enable us to understand the world and our place within it. What gives us such abilities is the same thing that creates self-consciousness.

So, what do we mean by 'Consciousness' and why has it been called 'The Hard Problem', a phrase put forward by philosopher David Chalmers in 'The Conscious Mind (1996)? The book explores various theories and approaches to consciousness, questioning how subjective experiences can arise from physical processes. An example is touching a red-hot surface; the biological process would immediately signal the brain, triggering a chain of events in which our nerve endings detect harm and send a signal to the brain. The brain then processes the information as pain, and we experience the subjective conscious reaction to feeling pain.

In a nutshell, consciousness is our ability to have inner experiences and feel sensations. While we cannot directly observe ourselves, we can observe the effects of our emotions on others. We understand that our thoughts give rise to feelings and that there is an external world beyond our inner one.

The Hard Problem, which no one in the scientific or any other field fully understands, is how physical processes can create a subjective experience or how the brain can generate consciousness, thereby promoting in us an emotional experience such as pain. One difficulty is that each of us has unique experiences, making direct observation a challenging task. Feedback relies on self-reporting, which we know can be influenced by biases, culture, and religion, all aspects of human conditioning.

Interestingly, the true challenge lies in the gap between the objective, observable world of science and the subjective realm of personal experience. It is, of course, the same question that emerges from studies concerning metaphysical experiences and the afterlife.

So, if we see consciousness as that which makes us feel alive and allows us to experience the world through our thoughts and emotions, or, as some are now proposing, could it be that consciousness doesn't live in the brain at all but exists outside of the brain and we draw from its energy? The consensus in the scientific realm, however, is that consciousness ceases to exist once the brain is dead and argues that there is no empirical evidence to support the idea that consciousness lives on beyond the point of clinical death.

Dr Peter Fenwick's 'The Art of Dying' (2008) rejects this view after studying NDEs, the human brain, and the question of consciousness for over 50 years. Acknowledging his scepticism, the neuropsychiatrist argues that his research suggests that consciousness continues after death.

The spiritual belief that we are all part of one universe, that we are all energy, and that we return to the universal energy upon our material death lends itself to Fenwick's belief that our consciousness returns to the cosmic consciousness and lives on. It also explains why we cannot measure it by any scientific method, so, if this proves accurate, will the 'hard problem' ever be solvable? The good news is that the debate has been open for centuries and shows no signs of slowing down. Perhaps we may find the answer if we become less conditioned and more free-thinking.

As stated earlier, we are fascinated by the idea of a paranormal world that goes beyond what we can see, feel, and observe easily, but that raises the question. 'What is reality, existence, and consciousness? It backs up the spiritual perspective of an afterlife and the interconnectedness of all things. This offers us a purpose and a sense of meaning in life, opening the mysteries of the unknown and allowing for more profound insights into the Universe and the question, 'Who Am I?'

The scientific standpoint views consciousness as closely linked to the activity of neurons and the brain's functioning. This perspective suggests that thoughts, perceptions, and experiences are nothing more than interactions within the brain, created by electrical signals and chemical reactions that continually occur. To that extent, neuroscientists have made significant strides in identifying brain regions involved in aspects of consciousness, including sensory perception, decision-making, and self-awareness. By looking at brain injuries and altered states of consciousness, including meditation, hypnosis and psychedelic drugs, they can pinpoint which areas of the brain have been affected. They still cannot answer the question of what consciousness is.

The suggestion is that consciousness is brain-based, and changes in the brain's activity can lead to changes in consciousness. This would rule out the question of consciousness being external and transferable, existing outside of the brain. It doesn't give us a credible explanation of phenomena such as out-of-body experiences or Near-Death experiences.

Is it then that consciousness exists both internally aligned to functions in our brain and externally related to the universal whole? Indeed, in Eastern philosophy, the belief is that consciousness is interconnected with the universe, a oneness with everything. This gives rise to an extended consciousness transcending the human brain. Indeed, there is considerable evidence to support this idea.

Dr. Oliver Lazar, in his book 'Beyond Matter' (2023), is a professor and scientist who was usually involved in research of the material world until, in 2017, he witnessed the fatal accident of his daughter's friend and felt a great empathy and connection which he could not explain or get rid of. Then, several weeks later, he experienced what he describes as a spiritual awakening. He describes his body becoming flooded with an overwhelming feeling of love and joy. This experience led him to research everything mystical. He also began to meditate, and as he recognised, he was feeling consciousness from the outside and not the inside, his life changed totally, along with his belief that consciousness survives the death of the body.

The philosophical field of Panpsychism, now gaining attention, suggests that consciousness is a fundamental aspect of the universe and that all entities on Earth possess some form of consciousness, not limited to just the human species and animals.

Many religions propose the existence of an afterlife, which suggests some form of continued consciousness. This is undoubtedly the case with Christianity. Hinduism and Buddhism believe in reincarnation, implying a cycle of rebirth and, therefore, a continued existence of consciousness. Whilst such beliefs are deeply entrenched in religion and some fields of philosophy, scientists argue that the existence of consciousness beyond the human body is highly speculative and cannot be measured using rigid scientific methods. However, it remains a topic of ongoing exploration. To date, no conclusive scientific evidence of the afterlife has been found.

Regardless of one's beliefs, the role of consciousness in understanding metaphysical experiences and the afterlife is fundamental. There are many diverse opinions on what constitutes reality and what does not. Whether consciousness is universal or a product of the mind's interconnections, maintaining an open mind to all possibilities is essential if the hard question is ever to be fully answered.

In the words of Manly P Hall, 'The Secret Teachings of All Ages' (1968), 'It is difficult for the human mind to acknowledge that which it doesn't understand. We are conditioned to think logically rather than expand the boundaries of our knowledge.'

Could our intellect be too limited to understand what we cannot logically see? Is this the fundamental riddle of consciousness? We agreed that consciousness remains a complex puzzle, with many pieces still missing. A definitive conclusion about what consciousness is eludes us, but hopefully, through ongoing research with an open mind, we will answer one day.

> There is no doubt that consciousness is the most puzzling and important aspect of our lives
> David Chalmers

4. A Glimpse of the Other Side (NDEs)

Does consciousness exist after death? If the answer is yes, then it would suggest that there is an afterlife, a place where our soul goes. Irrespective of your views on the question, near-death experiences (NDEs) would appear to confirm that there is something beyond that which we call mortal death.

A firm advocate of this view of consciousness is Dr. Peter Fenwick, a British Neuropsychiatrist who, in his book, 'The Truth in the Light' 1995, persuasively argues that his findings suggest that consciousness does exist beyond physical death. He further states that we are all interconnected as a unified energy that merges back into a cosmic consciousness upon death. f

Co-authored with his wife, Elizabeth, he analysed over 300 NDE experience accounts and found recurring patterns such as a feeling of peace and being out of the body. Travelling through a tunnel, seeing a bright light, meeting deceased relatives, a life review and being told to return, it was not their time.

So, what do we mean by NDE? Many definitions are provided in various books and articles. Although the wording may differ slightly, there is a consensus on the main aspects of such an experience.

An NDE is seen to be a deep personal encounter, often associated with a life-threatening situation in which a person feared that they were dying or would die. This could be following an accident, cardiac arrest, or a critical situation. It occurs when an individual has been declared clinically dead but later revived.

Many aspects of NDE reports concur with those of Fenwick, involving a journey taken at lightning speed, bright lights, meeting with deceased relatives, and an overwhelming feeling of love.

One of the first stories I was told when writing this book was that of Paul, a retired 71-year-old engineer. These are his words:

'I was told I had prostate cancer and needed urgent surgery. I had lost weight and noticed difficulty when

urinating but never suspected cancer. I felt overwhelmed and just wanted the thing out. I hated hospitals, but not as much as I hated the thought that I had something inside of me eating me away. The next few weeks went by in a blur of family tears and fear. Then, there I was in the hospital being prepared for surgery. The last thing I remembered was being told to count from 100 down, everything went black, and then I found myself up on the ceiling of the operating room looking down at myself. I should have felt terrified, but I didn't. I was watching them pumping my chest, and I could see with their faces that something had gone wrong. People were dashing in and out of the room, and I saw the consultant shake his head.

Next minute, I was in the dark, and the chaos in the theatre had stopped. I felt peaceful; everything was black, but I had no fear. Then I heard a whooshing sound and was pulled upward at speed. I saw things that had happened in my life, but I also felt how my actions had affected others. I was then in the open, in bright light, and I couldn't see anything, but I felt this immense feeling of love. I just wanted to be there, but knew I wasn't meant to stay. In one instance, I was back in my own body. The first thing I became aware of was the loud buzz of instruments and a feeling of pain in my body.

I'm from a family of atheists, as I was before this happened. I would have been ridiculed if I had spoken out then, so I kept quiet but never forgot. I'm sure I died that day, and I know I changed as a person. When I finally did tell my family, they laughed at me and said I'd had too much of the anaesthetic and was dreaming. At that time, I knew nothing about NDEs. Still, since I have done a lot of reading and recognise hundreds, even thousands of people have had what I had, so now I don't care what people think, I know there is something after we leave this life."

Has it given me a sense of a higher purpose in life? I now love studying and having time to reflect, which I never made time for before my NDE. I am more aware of what is happening around me than ever before, and I see things differently. I suppose having cancer makes you think differently about life, but it's more than that. I can't explain it; I feel different in some way. Little things that annoyed me once don't matter anymore.

I increasingly feel like an observer rather than an active participant, especially about trivial matters. Many issues I once considered worth debating, sometimes heatedly, now seem unimportant. I realise how easily we get caught up in disagreements over small things and lose sight of what genuinely matters. Life is too precious to waste on unimportant squabbles, and I'm learning to experience the moments that genuinely give me fulfilment.'

Near-death experiences (NDEs) are not a new phenomenon; they are reported by both adults and children as far back as Plato and the bible and beyond. As noted under Historical Revelations and Beliefs, there have always been accounts of what we now refer to as near-death experiences (NDEs). Hadith literature tells of the Prophet Muhammad ascending to heaven, meeting prophets and witnessing paradise before returning to life.

When we compare the elements of ancient descriptions of what we now call near-death experiences (NDEs) across various traditions, it becomes evident that specific themes are common. These include out-of-body experiences, journeys to other realms, encounters with spiritual beings, life reviews, and a return to life accompanied by a profound message.

Dr. Raymond Moody coined the term "near-death experience" in his 1975 book 'Life After Life.' This publication sparked extensive research into the topic, which continues to this day. I purchased this book when it was released, and it still sits on my bookshelf, the first in my ever-growing collection of books on metaphysical experience.

Many people worldwide have shared their stories of near-death experiences (NDEs), and these tales have stirred our imagination. In these remarkable moments, individuals often describe profound changes in their perception of life, sharing vivid and sometimes surreal experiences they encountered during critical situations. With the rise of social media, numerous personal accounts are now available, making it easier to explore the phenomenon of near-death experiences (NDEs).

A common thread, as noted above, emerges in these experiences: many people report overwhelming feelings of love, acceptance, and warmth. Some describe the sensation of floating outside their bodies, while others recount encounters with deceased loved ones or experiences involving glowing beings. These experiences can profoundly alter how individuals perceive their lives once they return to the everyday world. The growing interest in NDEs underscores our deep curiosity about life, death, and what may lie beyond.

Numerous resources are available if you're interested in learning more about this topic. You can find academic studies, books written by people who have had NDEs, and online forums where people share their thoughts and experiences. These insights can help you gain a deeper understanding of the complex relationship between consciousness and our human experience. It might even bring some comfort and hope as you ponder the big questions in life.

There are so many books and personal stories about near-death experiences (NDEs) that it can be hard to keep track of them all. Some researchers think that consciousness might extend beyond the body. In contrast, others believe that these experiences are just the brain reacting as we near death, influenced by physical and psychological factors. Despite all the discussion, no one has been able to prove exactly what NDEs are. One thing is clear: the many thousands of people who have gone through these experiences are convinced that what they felt was real, and nothing will change their minds about it.

Anyone wishing to read about these fascinating experiences can visit the website of Dr. Jefferey Long, a leading researcher on NDEs who has devoted a lifetime to understanding them. As a result of his research, he developed the NDERF (Near Death Experience Research Foundation) site, which has the first-hand accounts of thousands of people who have experienced an NDE and is the largest site of its kind in the world. Another helpful site is that of IANDS (International Association for Near-Death Experiences), which underwent a complete overhaul in 2025. IANDS was founded in 1978 by a group of researchers investigating near-death experiences (NDEs). One of whom was Dr Bruce Greyson, an avid author of books on NDEs.

One story from the IANDS site features Shannon, an ICU nurse, and offers a different perspective on NDEs. Shannon tells the story of John, who had recently undergone open-heart surgery. She responded to a code bell going off during the night shift. Hurrying into the patient's room, she found him sitting in a chair, unresponsive. He had stopped breathing and was flatlining. Along with other nurses, CPR started, followed by shocking him back to life. John's eyes had been closed throughout the experience. Shannon was not John's nurse, nor had she met him before this event. This is her account of what happened next, days after she went to check on his welfare.

'You don't remember me, but I was here the night that you coded, and your heart stopped.'

His reply confused Shannon.

'I know you were here; you were the one who shocked me. You were standing right here.'

John pointed to the exact spot Shannon was standing on when she shocked him. He then told her.

'I was watching you from up there. I was just observing and was at complete peace. I thought you were going to burn my ripples when you shocked me.'

Shannon was astonished to learn that John could observe events from the ceiling while clinically dead. A decade later, she clearly remembers him and believes death is not the end. This is her account of the experience.

'There is some sort of transformation in which consciousness continues without the physical body. When this happens, there is no pain. There is no fear. Just an overwhelming sense of peace. Your thoughts remain your own, but the negative aspects of the physical world are no longer present. I wouldn't trade this experience for anything in the world. Thanks, John.'

What's interesting about this experience is that it's something shared between two people and profoundly changes what both believe. One person has a near-death experience (NDE), while the other witnesses it.

For the person who has the NDE, this can be a life-changing event. John came back with new ideas about life and death; he was less afraid of dying and more connected to everything around him. On the other hand, Shannon, who didn't have the NDE, is also affected. After experiencing her conversation with John, she is now a believer in the afterlife.

One of the earliest published studies of NDEs, although not known by that name at the time, was in 1892 when a Swiss geologist, Albert Heim, documented accounts from over thirty individuals who had survived near-death experiences. His study included climbers who had fallen from heights, soldiers wounded in battle, and victims of accidents such as near-drownings. In his work "Remarks on Fatal Falls," he recounts how individuals shared vivid experiences during the critical moments, which included a life review, the absence of pain, visions of beauty, and a slowing down of time. Heim's work was prompted by his brush with death in a harrowing fall while mountaineering and laid the groundwork for further research into NDEs.

Many books on near-death experiences (NDEs) today are written by individuals who have had such an experience and are deeply affected, inspiring them to explore the subject further. Eben Alexander is a prime example of this. Dr Paul Kalanithi's 'When Breath Becomes Air' (2016) was also a neurosurgeon who became the patient when diagnosed with terminal cancer. Although he doesn't discuss NDEs, his book offers profound insights into mortality and the meaning of life from both medical and personal viewpoints.

There is no scarcity of material for research into Near-Death Experiences (NDEs). The same is true for the numerous personal accounts available to read, such as that of Renee Judkins, who suffered from stage 4 rectal cancer and was given only a few months to live.

During one of her week-long chemotherapy treatments, Renee died and describes how she crossed over from the physical realm into the non-physical. She states:

'There were no bright lights or dead relatives. I did feel as though I passed through some sort of portal, though. There was an overwhelming feeling of warmth and unconditional love. There were many souls to greet me there, some I recognised, others I did not know in physical life.'

She continues to discuss how all communication was telepathic and how she sensed rather than saw these beings. Unlike others, Renee was made aware of what she called many truths. These were conveyed to her directly from what we might refer to as 'God', to use a name. This is what she states:

'Of the truths I learned there, the most important one I wish to share with you is this: there is NO religion in the non-physical. Infinite intelligence, All That is, God, if you will. This infinite intelligence does not recognise or acknowledge bad, wrong, evil or sin, no need for forgiveness, no need to be 'saved'. We…. You are an extension of Source Energy, an extension of the same energy.'

While most NDEs report positive effects like peace, light, and unconditional love, a smaller but notable number of cases describe distressing or frightening events.

Christopher was an atheist who had an NDE in 1985. Instead of experiencing peace and love, he described seeing and being guided by shadowy figures to a dark place where he was mocked and emotionally tormented. He felt engulfed by complete hopelessness until he called out for divine help. A bright light saved him, and from that moment, his experience followed the more traditional NDE pattern. The experience changed his beliefs and how he has lived his life since.

A similar case involved a woman named Clara, who had a life-saving operation and reported experiencing a very disturbing NDE.

'There was no light, I was in pitch darkness. I knew that there were things around me, and I felt I was being prodded and pushed. I was in total despair. It was as if I were nothing but my thoughts until I found myself back in my body.'

Detailed in Time Magazine (Aug 2016), Dr Rajiv Parti, formerly a chief anaesthesiologist, underwent emergency surgery in 2010 and recounted having an NDE in which he visited what he described as a 'Hellish Realm.' During his time there, he was made to contemplate the consequences of his materialistic and self-centered life. The revelations caused him to experience deep remorse, and he felt a sense of spiritual emptiness.

What is remarkable about all near-death experiences (NDEs) is the profound transformation that occurs in the individual experiencing them. In most cases, whether the experience is positive or negative, the outcome is the same: a move away from a materialistic way of life towards a more spiritual existence.

While most NDEs focus on adult experiences, NDERF (Near Death Experience Research Foundation) documents many accounts provided by children. One young girl, just 2 years old, suffered a sudden cardiac arrest and was clinically dead for four minutes before being resuscitated. Several months later, she told her older sister that God told her she would be better while he was carrying her into the sky before putting her back in her body.

Another young girl, only four years old, recounted her journey through a tunnel filled with light and her arrival in a place she called 'home.' She described the area as being encircled by a luminous field and a large oak tree. She then explained how she had seen a nurse who had lost a ring, mentioning its location during the time she was out of her body. These were details she couldn't have known during her resuscitation.

Sally, aged 10, nearly drowned while wading in a river near her family's log cabin. During her NDE, she felt enveloped by a radiant light and described the sensation as being 'home.' She spoke of the water's clarity and the sense of peace she felt.

The feeling of being overwhelmed by love and extreme peacefulness is a strong feature in most NDEs. While children may have limitations in language to explain their experiences, many of the characteristics they display are shared by adult accounts. As with adults, the stages are similar, with one noticeable difference: child accounts do not mention life reviews.

Dr. Bruce Greyson, co-founder of IANDS, regarded NDEs as intensely vivid and often life-changing experiences that typically follow a recognisable pattern of events, including features such as:

Clarity and speed of thinking increase.
A sense of overwhelming unconditional love.
Freedom from pain.
Out-of-body experience.
Being drawn into a tunnel.
A brilliant light or being of light.
Life Review.

Seeing deceased loved ones.
Things that are generally not known.
Decision to stay or return.

Among the many reports I have studied, it becomes clear that not only do those who experience NDEs give similar accounts of the stages they go through, but also of the after-effects of the experience. All state that they no longer have any fear of death. Their attitudes towards others become more empathetic and loving. A sense of compassion and acceptance of others is felt, along with an increased sense of life's meaning. Material possessions, status, and the need to compete become less appealing. This remains true even where the experiencer was an atheist.

What is also clear about NDEs is that, for the person experiencing one, it feels genuine and significant. Although there is no scientific method to confirm or disprove whether death is the end definitively, it is acknowledged that such experiences are increasingly being reported. Moreover, there is a rising interest among scholars in investigating this subject.

So, is there evidence suggesting that NDEs are genuinely real? Several researchers, including Dr Pim van Lommel, Dr Bruce Greyson, and Dr Sam Parnia, have observed that the memories of those who experienced an NDE remained consistent over time. This implies that the experience was authentic and not fabricated. Additionally, NDEs are not uncommon, and various surveys indicate that between 4% and 20% of people resuscitated after a cardiac arrest report having such an experience.

Can we keep ignoring the thousands of NDEs reported as not scientifically proven and therefore not real? When examining the evidence, it is convincing. For example, how can someone provide precise details of their operation, who was present, what was said, and what happened when they are clinically dead with tape over their eyes? Why do near-death experiences (NDEs) share similar characteristics across the globe? How can individuals recognise people they have seen during their NDE but have never met in real life? Why is it that children who have experienced NDES can retell them using more descriptive language than expected for their age? And why do those who have had NDEs report significant changes in their beliefs and lifestyle afterwards?

The subject of near-death experiences (NDEs) remains highly debated, with opinions constantly shifting as new research emerges. For those who have undergone an NDE, however, their experiences seem intensely real and meaningful. Many of them leave with a strong belief that life is precious and must be treasured.

People who have experienced these moments often describe feelings of love, a sense of connection with others, and a deeper understanding of what truly matters in life. These realisations cause them to value each day even more.

Conversely, scientists and researchers hold diverse views on NDEs. Some are keen to explore them further to understand how our brains and bodies react during such intense moments, while others argue that these experiences can be explained by the brain's responses to trauma or stress. As more studies are carried out and differing opinions arise, the discussion surrounding near-death experiences (NDEs) becomes increasingly intricate.

Ultimately, discussing NDEs raises essential questions about life, death, and what it means to be human. It prompts us to reflect on our existence and the mysteries that go beyond our current understanding of life.

5. Do Guardian Angels Guide Us?

The belief in angels as real spiritual beings is not a new idea. In many religions and cultures, angels are viewed as non-physical beings created by a higher power whose purpose is to guide and help humanity. Their role is seen as that of guardians sent to protect us and lead us through life's challenges. But do they really exist? They certainly remain unproven; however, there is no evidence to disprove their existence either.

Sceptics argue that angels do not exist and that encounters with them are simply coincidental events. They propose that these experiences are forms of wishful thinking or psychological projections, where the idea of an angel reflects an external expression of a deeply held inner conviction. For example, someone with a strong desire for protection might project the presence of a guardian angel meant to keep them safe. This belief eases their fears of feeling unprotected, rather than confirming the actual existence of a guardian angel.

It is undeniable, however, that this area has fascinated humanity for a millennium. In many religious traditions, guardian angels are regarded as divine messengers or protectors assigned to individuals. They are well-established in the Christian faith, particularly in Catholicism. Does the Bible not tell us of the angel Gabriel's visit to Mary, announcing to her that she is to have a child conceived by the Holy Spirit? (Luke 1:26) Is it not an angel that rolls away the stone from Jesus's tomb and announces his resurrection? (Matthew 28:2). We also see two angels warning Lot about the destruction of Sodom and Gomorrah (Genesis 32:24). In the Quran, it is the Angel Jibril (Gabriel) who reveals the Quran to Muhammad. (Surah Al-Baqarah 2:97). The book of Enoch (a Jewish apocryphal text) recounts angels who have roles in the judgement and guidance of humanity.

Regardless of belief, it is widely accepted that people find comfort in the idea of guardian angels, whether in a spiritual context or as human beings they call Earth Angels. So, what distinguishes heavenly angels from Earth Angels?

Earth Angels are often described as individuals with exceptional kindness, compassion, and a strong desire to help others. They are not supernatural beings but humans whose behaviour and traits distinguish them. These individuals are seen as being deeply linked to the spiritual realm, displaying qualities that inspire goodness and positivity in those around them.

Earth Angels often feel a strong calling to improve the world. They might take part in humanitarian work, counselling, or spiritual practices. They are thought to have heightened empathy and intuition, helping them understand and support others on a deeply emotional level. The term "Earth Angel" is metaphorical, symbolising their role as a beacon of hope, love, and healing in the physical world.

Key Characteristics of Earth Angels

Human Origin: Earth Angels are ordinary people who exhibit extraordinary qualities.

Empathy and Compassion: They have a deep understanding of others' emotions and often feel compelled to help.

Connection to Spirituality: Many Earth Angels believe in and practice spiritual principles to guide their actions and intentions.

Desire for Positive Change: They often work to uplift humanity and contribute to societal well-being.

Nurses are often described as 'Earth Angels' and regarded as individuals with exceptional qualities of kindness, compassion, and a strong desire to help others. They are not supernatural beings; instead, they are humans whose behaviours and traits distinguish them.

These individuals are seen as being deeply connected to the spiritual realm, demonstrating qualities that inspire goodness and positivity in those around them. Florence Nightingale was a British nurse who cared for soldiers during the Crimean War. She was also an advocate for social reform, which led to the revolutionisation of nursing practices. Nurses became known as angels on earth to many of the wounded men they cared for.

Spiritual Angels, on the other hand, are thought to be non-physical, supernatural entities believed to exist in the spiritual realm. Unlike Earth Angels, Spiritual Angels are not human but are regarded as celestial beings who support humanity through intervention, guidance, or inspiration.

Key Characteristics of Spiritual Angels

Divine Origin: Spiritual Angels are supernatural beings created by a higher power.

Non-Physical Forms: They are believed to exist in realms beyond the physical world.

Roles in Guidance: Spiritual Angels act as protectors, messengers, or guides for humanity.

Presence in Religious Texts: Many major religions describe angels and their roles in sacred writings.

Although Earth Angels and Spiritual Angels share the same purpose of guiding and helping humanity, they differ significantly in their nature and origin.

Earth Angels and Spiritual Angels embody two distinct yet complementary notions of goodness and guidance. While Earth Angels inspire others through human connection and kindness, Spiritual Angels offer divine assistance and protection from realms beyond our understanding. Together, they symbolise humanity's lasting faith in the power of love, hope, and spiritual guidance.

Numerous accounts of angels have been documented, with one of the most enduring legends being that of the Angels of Mons. This story dates to World War I and is said to have taken place during the Battle of Mons, when British soldiers reported witnessing angelic beings allegedly protecting them. Many dismissed this as mass hysteria in the face of death or wartime propaganda. Although many soldiers died that day, others who survived provided eyewitness accounts of the event.

Accounts of angels are numerous, with the Angels of Mons being a well-known legend from World War I. During the Battle of Mons, British soldiers reported seeing angelic beings protecting them. This was often dismissed as wartime propaganda or mass hysteria. Despite many casualties, survivors offered eyewitness accounts of the battle.

The British were reportedly outnumbered and faced a strong German offensive. Logically, the platoon should have been overwhelmed, but instead, they inflicted significant casualties on the Germans, believing they were being protected. After the battle, stories spread widely about how the men had been saved through supernatural forces. This underscores the human need for meaning, protection, and hope amid overwhelming danger. Whether seen as divine intervention or the product of imagination, we cannot escape its influence over beliefs.

I wonder how many have watched 'It's a Wonderful Life', a film that is a firm favourite at Christmas. It tells the story of a man who wants to end his life, but an intervention by an angel, seeking to earn its wings, makes him realise how important his life has been and will continue to be. It's a feel-good film, like 'Touched by an Angel, where these celestial beings, often portrayed in human form, act as compassionate guides.

Angels are believed to infiltrate and influence cultures. They permeate literature, films, popular writings, music, and poetry. This is evident with writers like Jacky Newcomb, known as the angel lady. Jacky is a renowned author of books such as 'An Angel by My Side' (2006) and 'Angels Watching Over Me' (2007). She has also appeared on many radio shows; notably, she was a guest alongside Tony Blair. The host invited listeners to call in with questions for both guests. Within minutes, the lines were overwhelmed with questions for Jacky, and Tony Blair, the Prime Minister, was forgotten. Such is the power of belief.

In both books I have mentioned, numerous accounts describe encounters with angels and spiritual beings, usually during life-threatening situations. These stories include miraculous escapes and rescues by strangers often perceived as angels in disguise. Dream visitations convey essential messages to the recipient, and many accounts from children detail encounters with angels and stories of pets returning to earth to protect their owners.

During my time as a mind-body coach, I met a client who shared an experience that happened when she moved into a new house. Shortly after arriving, her young daughter asked her about the lady who had visited her when she was in bed. Concerned, my client asked for more details. Her daughter described a woman who never spoke but was always smiling. The girl was unafraid and said the woman was kind. Research into the house revealed that the previous owner had a mother who died in the bedroom where the child slept. After the girl's questions, the woman never appeared again.

There was a time when I lost both my father and my brother in quick succession, and the grief was overwhelming. Not long after each of their deaths, I had separate experiences where I saw them by my bedside. Both times, it felt like they were letting me know they were alright, and somehow, I found comfort in that. I've often wondered if this was just wishful thinking on my part, a result of mourning, but honestly, I don't think so. The way they appeared to me was so vivid and real, nothing like any dream I've ever had before or since. The sense of peace and reassurance I felt stayed with me long afterwards, and it made me believe that, in some way, they were reaching out to let me know everything was alright.

While on a bus journey, I spoke with a stranger about writing this book. She shared a story about her uncle, who was dying of terminal cancer. She had been scheduled to marry just two days after visiting him, having been told that he only had a few days to live. As she was about to leave his bedside, he unexpectedly grasped her hand and urged her not to marry the boy. Intriguingly, this was a boy he had never met, and she hadn't discussed him in much detail with her uncle. Despite his warning, the marriage went ahead, and her new husband turned out to be an abuser. They separated several months later. How could her uncle have possibly foreseen her future?

I have heard so many stories about metaphysical experiences during my discussions about the book that it would require a new book to tell them all. Many of those stories include warnings or involving children.

It has led me to question why children might be more prone to seeing spiritual beings than adults. Is it because they have less social conditioning and therefore do not dismiss such experiences as incompatible with rational thought? Could children be more spiritually receptive, having not been indoctrinated with scientific reasoning and methodology? Perhaps they do not need evidence to believe in something beyond what we know. Or is it that they have more vivid imaginations and less developed critical thinking skills?

In her book 'An Angel by my Side', Jacky Newsome recounts the story of a twenty-month-old girl who spoke of someone who blew her kisses. Her mother wondered if it might be her mother, who had passed away before the child's birth, but knew about the pregnancy. As the little girl developed her verbal skills, her mother often heard whispering from the nursery intercom. The whispers came from two voices, but whenever the mother checked on her daughter, she found the child pointing to the corner of the room.

Kyle Gray is a well-known spiritual teacher and is regarded as an angel expert, offering a contemporary guide on how to connect with angels and recognise signs that they are near. 'Angels are with You Now.' (2025) is part of the new wave of books that explore spiritual healing and self-empowerment. In line with the New Age movement, the book emphasises spiritual growth and self-development.

Angels in the New Age Movement are seen as non-judgmental beings of light who guide, protect, and support us along our life's journey. New Age angels can be contacted through prayer, meditation, or by tuning into their presence intuitively. They are often described as energy, vibrations, and colours that can help heal and reassure individuals during challenging times and life changes. Their beliefs aim to remove the dogma surrounding metaphysical experiences.

Besides books, websites offering angel card readings and sites dedicated to individual accounts, numerous blogs and YouTube videos now exist, featuring posts from people who wish to discuss or share their own experiences. These sites attract thousands of followers. We should ask ourselves WHY? Is it because humanity longs for hope and an end to suffering, or is it mass delusion?

Several of the accounts sourced from websites and YouTube share an ordinary subject matter. The central theme revolves around survival and being rescued by angels. One man recounted how he was walking near a construction site and, without understanding why, he suddenly stopped. A heavy beam landed just in front of him, missing him by inches. He had felt an intense pressure on his shoulder before stopping and believed it was a guardian angel.

A young girl trapped in a house fire reported hearing calm, reassuring voices guiding her through the building to an open window, where firefighters then rescued her. She said the voice wasn't one she recognised or had heard before, and it was so sweet that it stopped her from panicking. Her parents are convinced this was a guardian angel.

In another account, a man driving in icy conditions lost control of his car and ended up in a ditch. Before he could call for help, a stranger in a bright coat appeared and helped him out of the car, reassuring him that he would be okay. Minutes later, emergency services arrived, but there was no sign of the man in the bright coat, nor were there any footprints in the snow.

Edwin was eighty-seven years old and nearing the end of his life. He then began to report that little, blonde-haired boys were sitting on his bed at night, comforting him. He had no fear but was confused as to where these children were coming from. His family was sure they were angels waiting for him.

Lily was facing a severe illness and a traumatic period in her life when she reached the breaking point and took an overdose. While waiting for the ambulance, her husband described how she stared into a corner of the room and began speaking to her deceased parents, telling them she was ready to go. She then started smiling and nodding before looking at her husband and saying she would be alright now. She recovered from both her illness and depression.

Dream warnings are also common, and there have been several well-documented reports of people experiencing them. Indeed, President Abraham Lincoln reportedly had a vivid dream in which he saw his funeral. Upon asking a guard who had died, he was told the President had been assassinated. He was assassinated shortly afterwards.

Eryl Mai Jones, a ten-year-old girl from the village of Aberfan, told her mother she had dreamed that her school was buried by something black. The next day, the Aberfan disaster happened, and the village school was buried beneath a collapsing coal tip. One hundred and sixteen children and 28 adults lost their lives. Eryl was among the dead.

We refer to these experiences as Premonition Dreams, where an unknown force seems to warn us of an impending disaster affecting ourselves or others. While scientists often dismiss these dreams as mere coincidences, does that truly explain their detailed accuracy? Are we being visited by angels, warning us of danger? Ultimately, they remain a mystery that science has yet to unravel.

An area that is gaining increased recognition is palliative and hospice care. This interest arises from frequent encounters with terminally ill patients, both young and old, who report experiencing angelic and otherworldly figures. Family members and medical staff see these as angels visiting and supporting patients on their journey to a new existence. In one paediatric hospice, a nurse recounted a story about a young boy who told her that angels were singing and telling him not to be scared. A mother shared that her young son saw an angel with large golden wings in the room just before he passed away. Numerous similar accounts appear throughout the literature involving angels.

Dr. Elisabeth Kübler-Ross was recognised as one of the world's leading experts on death, dying, and the afterlife. She dedicated many years to studying and working with those who were terminally ill. She often stated that it was through these experiences that she learned the importance of life. In her 1991 book, "On Life After Death," Kübler-Ross details the extensive research she conducted over the years, which included cases from various countries such as the USA, Australia, and Canada, covering diverse religious and cultural backgrounds like Aboriginals, Hindus, Buddhists, Jews, and individuals with no religious beliefs. Her studies also explored near-death experiences (NDEs). While she acknowledges that scientists and sceptics often dismiss her findings as "wishful thinking," she raises an intriguing question: How can blind people describe colours and details from a room they were in during their experience?

In her book 'On Children and Death' (1983), Kubler-Ross examines terminal illness in children. The book is regarded as a compassionate work that has supported many parents who have lost their young ones. She emphasises that even very young children can sense when they are dying and are highly intuitive. They do not experience feelings of denial and often comfort their parents by claiming to have seen angels, past relatives, and bright lights, telling them not to worry any longer.

Hospice workers often report that children describe seeing "shining people" or individuals with wings who are waiting for them. These children typically pass away shortly after making these observations. A notable case is that of Joseth, a six-year-old boy who was hospitalised with pneumonia. He told his parents about a 'beautiful glowing lady' at the end of his bed. Joseth described the lady as holding his hand and reassured him that he would be alright. Remarkably, he recovered despite his critical condition.

Children often share mesmerising experiences filled with vivid imagery that ignites the imagination. They describe glowing figures that fill the air with warmth, lights that dance in bright colours, and ethereal wings that flutter. These experiences are often accompanied by a sense of love, creating a safe space where worries seem to fade away.

In these moments, children may report hearing sweet singing that fills their hearts, bringing feelings of joy and oneness. Often, they describe a deep sense of peace as they feel the presence of comforting figures, which they perceive as angels. These beings, they say, communicate but without using words, conveying understanding and reassurance simply through their presence.

The recurring themes of companionship and unconditional love are powerful, emphasising the innocence and wonder of childhood. This mixture of imagination and spirituality helps children to grasp deeper emotions. It gives them a sense of security, reminding us of the beautiful simplicity of their world.

What evidence exists for the existence of guardian angels? While there is no scientific proof, like most metaphysical experiences, does this mean it's simply wishful thinking, or could there be something beyond our current understanding? Might we have silent helpers? Beliefs in guardian angels have persisted across cultures for many years, supported by reports from children, medical professionals, and everyday individuals.

The extensive collection of personal testimonies and anecdotal evidence is striking, as shown by their widespread presence in both literature and media. These stories offer unique insights into human experiences and have played a vital role in shaping public opinion on various issues. The importance of these accounts has not been overlooked, leading to numerous studies conducted by respected experts across multiple fields. Can we dismiss this increasing interest as simply a human need for guidance and safety?

6. Multiple Lives, Multiple Journeys

The mystery of what happens after our death has inspired many beliefs and spiritual traditions. One of the most intriguing ideas is that of Reincarnation, which has fascinated humans throughout history. The thought that the soul survives physical death and is reborn into new bodies or moves to different realms over multiple lifetimes is incredible. However, as with many metaphysical themes I have explored in this book, this belief is shared worldwide, from ancient India to classical Greece. Hinduism and Buddhism include reincarnation as a central part of their teachings. This is also reflected in the indigenous wisdom of modern spiritual movements, especially among New Age communities, which find comfort and meaning in the idea of having more than one life.

Reincarnation raises many vital questions about who we are, our consciousness, personal identity, karma, and the ultimate purpose of life. In this section, I aim to explore how the belief in rebirth has developed over time and its ongoing influence on modern cultures and individual lives.

Some fascinating studies have been conducted on children who claim to have lived different times and lives. Some of these accounts are uncanny, as the children share memories or knowledge that is difficult to explain. Their stories encourage us to consider the possibility of reincarnation and offer insights into prodigy cases where young children display skills well beyond their years. One example is Mozart, who composed his first symphony at the age of eight and played the piano like an impresario from the age of four. Did he bring fragments of his past with him?

For many individuals, the concept of reincarnation alters how we perceive morality and our connections with others. They believe that the decisions we make in one life affect what we are meant to learn in the future. Regardless of personal beliefs, thinking about multiple lives prompts us to see life, death, and what lies beyond in a different way. It challenges us to consider the bigger picture and our purpose in life.

Not all beliefs are linked to religion; for many people, it is because they experience a strong feeling of having been somewhere before. Déjà vu, as we call it. It can feel like an unexplained connection to a particular time, place, or person. I have always felt a strong affinity for the Victorian era, which I first developed as a young child. I was taken to York for the first time by my father. I was about eight years old and had never heard the term 'Déjà vu,' nor would I have understood its meaning at that age.

My father wanted to stroll down the Shambles, a remarkably well-preserved medieval street in York dating back to the 14th century. As we approached the narrow, cobbled pathway lined with timber-framed buildings, an overwhelming wave of nostalgia washed over me. The warm, centuries-old architecture and the quaint shops evoked a deep sense of familiarity within me. It felt as though I was reconnecting with a forgotten part of myself, and I was reluctant to leave. Every time I visit York, this same longing arises. I have a deep appreciation for its rich history and vibrant atmosphere. This sentiment also extends to anything reminiscent of the Victorian era, capturing my imagination in a way that feels both timeless and profoundly personal.

Déjà vu originates from the French meaning 'already seen' and describes the strange, brief sensation that you have experienced something before, even when, as with my experience, you are witnessing it for the first time. Research into Déjà vu indicates that between 60% and 80% of people will encounter this phenomenon at some stage in their lives. Renowned experts have all tried to explain it, but it remains a mystery.

Numerous accounts exist of individuals experiencing a different life, many involving children who claim to remember a previous life. Children often begin talking about another life at a young age. They either forget it as they grow older or are discouraged from discussing it. William was only three years old when he started talking about his little brother, who lived with his other mummy. He described how he helped his mum care for his brother. He recounted how he had to work in a tall building when he was still young, though he didn't like it; however, he needed the money to support his family. By the age of four, his response to any questions was always the same: I don't want to talk about my brother; mummy says he is not real.

There is no doubt, however, that many accounts of past lives are fascinating. A well-documented case in India involved a young girl named Angelee, who spoke about her other family. She was four years old when the situation began. She recounted being married in a past life, describing the town where she had lived and providing details about her husband and children. Confused, her parents investigated and were alarmed to find that everything she had told them matched the life of a woman who had died nine years earlier.

A televised film was inspired by the life of Jenny Cockell, an English woman who had vivid dreams about her past life in Ireland, where she remembered her name as Mary Sutton. Jenny recalled that she had eight children and lived during the early 20th century. Through her research, she was able to locate the surviving children of Mary Sutton, who confirmed that her memories were accurate. Jenny shares her experience in her book, 'Yesterday's Children.'

Another well-documented case involves an American boy who started experiencing nightmares at a very young age. He consistently dreamed of being shot down in an aircraft. He provided detailed information about a World War II pilot, including the aircraft type, the names of his fellow pilots, and even the aircraft carrier from which he operated. The case was investigated by researcher Dr Jim Tucker, who has documented over 2500 cases of reincarnation. The details he provided were confirmed as accurate, despite James never having been exposed to them.

Dr Tucker, before: Children's Memories of Previous Lives' (2021), noted that children frequently display knowledge of events and individuals from a past life without any obvious source. Some cases included verifiable details about deceased people unfamiliar to the child's family. He concluded that there is a need for open-minded scientific research, which could provide insights into consciousness and its persistence beyond physical death.

Dr. Brian Weiss is an American psychiatrist who has authored several books on reincarnation. He supports regression therapy, which he believes can foster peace and healing. Weiss has shown that exploring past lives through regression can help to heal emotional and physical wounds in the present.

In his books 'Many Lives, Many Masters' (1988) and 'Same Soul, Many Bodies' (2004), he shares accounts of the regression sessions he has conducted with his patients, often taking them back to multiple past lives. His books have been translated into forty languages worldwide and have sold millions of copies. It is undeniable that there is a significant demand for 'knowing' and spiritual wisdom.

Weiss has worked with thousands of patients and has witnessed miraculous healing in those who have explored past lives to eliminate the emotional and physical barriers that cause illnesses, phobias, and fears. He recounts the story of a girl who developed a phobia of sharp objects at just eighteen months old and strongly disliked anyone touching her neck. It was revealed that in a past life, she had been a soldier who was speared in the neck and died after falling onto a sharp rock from her wound. Remarkably, her phobia was resolved immediately after she left his office.

Whether we believe in reincarnation or not, contemplating it can alter the way we view life. If we do return time and again, then life becomes more than just a brief journey from birth to death; it becomes part of a much larger story spanning multiple lifetimes. For some people, this idea offers comfort, implying that nothing is truly lost and that life serves a genuine purpose. We may start to feel that the obstacles we encounter, and the profound challenges are not punishments, but rather opportunities for us to learn and to be given chances to try again.

Reincarnation, much like near-death experiences (NDEs), can inspire compassion within us and serve as a guide for how we should live our daily lives. Similarly, the Tibetan Book of the Dead provides a framework for living in a way that allows the soul to continue its journey. Past life regression suggests that we can lead lives vastly differently from our current one; we may have experienced wealth or poverty, held power or felt powerless, and belonged to other races, nationalities, and genders. Compassion is gained by putting yourself into another person's shoes; perhaps this goes much deeper than thought.

The idea of living multiple lives provides comfort in knowing that our existence does not end with a single lifetime. It suggests that we continue our journey along different paths, offering hope during challenging times. Each life enables us to learn and develop, turning our difficulties into valuable lessons. This concept also emphasises our interconnectedness, as our experiences can influence others and enrich the shared human journey. Ultimately, embracing the idea of multiple lives empowers us to face life with resilience and curiosity, reminding us that our journey is ongoing.

There are many reasons against reincarnation, mainly the lack of scientific proof to support it. Reports of reincarnation cannot be reliably tested through the scientific method. Furthermore, many of these reports come from cultures where belief in reincarnation is widespread. Modern science considers memory and identity as functions of the physical brain; therefore, once the brain ceases to function, its memories are lost, making the idea of memory surviving across lifetimes unlikely.

The question arises as to how children can describe different lives in such detail and possess information that can later be verified. Additionally, why do some individuals have unusual birthmarks that correspond to a person they claim to have been in a past life? This aspect particularly intrigued Stevenson, especially when the marks matched autopsy or medical reports that confirmed their accuracy. This raises the question: can everything be proven scientifically? If not, does this suggest that research into past lives may have validity?

7. Out of Body Freedoms

**If the doors of perception were cleansed,
everything would appear to man as it is, infinite.
(William Blake)**

Out-of-body experiences (OBEs) are intriguing phenomena where individuals perceive themselves as viewing the world from a point outside their physical bodies. Many who have experienced an OBE describe floating above themselves, allowing them to look down and observe their bodies and surroundings from a different perspective. This experience can provoke a range of emotions, from wonder to fear, as it challenges our usual understanding of ourselves and consciousness.

OBEs can happen unexpectedly in various situations, but they can also be deliberately triggered using different methods. Common causes include intense emotional or physical trauma, high stress, meditation, or the use of certain drugs. Near-death experiences (NDEs), where individuals report similar sensations during severe health crises, are another context where OBEs frequently occur.

There are various types of OBEs. One common type occurs suddenly and unexpectedly, often when a person is resting or meditating. People describe these experiences as feeling as though they are hovering above themselves, usually accompanied by clear thoughts and heightened awareness. Another type, known as ceremonial-induced OBEs, happens in controlled environments where individuals use certain substances, such as hallucinogenic mushrooms, to modify their consciousness. These experiences can foster deep feelings of connection to something greater.

Both spontaneous and drug-induced OBEs raise intriguing questions about our minds and consciousness. While spontaneous OBEs may be beneficial during difficult times, ceremonial-induced ones often hold cultural and spiritual importance for personal growth. Ongoing research into OBEs could deepen our understanding of the nature of consciousness and our existence.

OBEs have a long history, with records from various cultures and religions that attest to this concept dating back well before scientific studies were conducted. For instance, in ancient Egypt, there was a belief in the 'Ka', regarded as a vital essence capable of leaving the body. In Hinduism, it is mentioned that the soul leaves and returns to the body. Simultaneously, yogis strongly believe in astral travel. Buddhism describes the 'Bardo', which refers to the state between death and rebirth. Monks recount their experiences of leaving the body during deep meditation. We hear of Shamans entering trance states to journey outside their bodies, typically to the spirit world. In Greek philosophy, Plato considered the idea of the soul's capacity to leave the body. Early Christianity includes stories of mystics like St. Teresa and Hildegard, who experienced visions in which their souls appeared to travel elsewhere.

In the 18th century, a man named Immanuel Swedenborg lived, who authored several books exploring the afterlife. 'Heaven and Hell' (1758) is his most renowned work. His writings were notable because Immanuel was a respected Swedish scientist and engineer. In 1744, he began to claim that he experienced dreams and visions that led to his spiritual awakening, during which he stated that God revealed to him the true nature of the afterlife. As a mystic, he greatly influenced individuals such as William Blake, Emerson, and Helen Keller, and a church was established in his name.

The Rosicrucian's, who still exist today, view Astral travel as a common voluntary Out-of-Body Experience (OBE). Moving into the 20th century, publications started to emerge about Astral Travel and OBEs. In the 1960s, a man named Robert Monroe, author of 'Journeys Out of the Body' (1971), began documenting spontaneous out-of-body experiences (OBEs) and coined the term 'Out-of-Body Experience.' He subsequently founded the Monroe Institute, which explores the idea that consciousness is not limited to the physical body. His interest arose from his own spontaneous out-of-body experiences, which he claimed occurred without any prior spiritual or mystical training.

Monroe describes these OBEs as events that often happen during his sleep or in an altered state of consciousness, featuring typical signs like a vibrating sensation, awareness of a second non-physical body, and travel to non-physical environments. It's important to emphasise that Monroe does not see OBEs as strange or mystical, but as a natural function of human consciousness that can be explored.

The following is a personal account by Robert Monroe of an OBE experience, taken from his work, 'Journeys Out of the Body'.

'I was lying in bed, not yet asleep, when I suddenly felt vibrations running through my body. The next moment, I was up near the ceiling, looking down at myself in bed. I could see the room clearly, including small details of a book I had left on the nightstand. I panicked and snapped back into my body with a jolt.'

Another spontaneous experience, from a UK study, involved a nine-year-old girl lying down on a sunny afternoon. She explained that she suddenly found herself hovering near the ceiling, looking down at herself. She wasn't frightened and said it felt natural. She watched the lights in the room and saw the patterns on the rug before being pulled back into her body.

A case documented in the European Journal of Parapsychology involved grief. After hearing news of a close friend's death, the man reported experiencing an out-of-body sensation. During this experience, he felt calm and contemplative about death. Nevertheless, he recognised that his body was overwhelmed by grief as he observed himself crying.

Meditation has long been used to induce out-of-body experiences (OBEs). As a meditation practitioner and teacher, I have worked with many clients, several of whom have reported feeling as if they are leaving their physical bodies. Rob, a believer in the power of the Universe, described feeling a sense of freedom while hovering above his body during our session. Ellen explained that she had felt as if she didn't belong in her body anymore.

Meditation is a widely recognised method for attaining different states of awareness. One of its primary benefits is the profound relaxation and peace that individuals experience after practising it. Indeed, in many spiritual traditions, OBEs are regarded as a natural phenomenon. You can find numerous meditation retreats in the UK that utilise breathwork to reach deep states of relaxation and induce OBEs and other spiritual experiences.

Experienced monks often describe entering a deep meditative state and becoming aware of leaving their bodies. They speak of travelling to different places and returning with vivid memories of the journeys. Invariably, these experiences are accompanied by feelings of comfort and peace, along with a sense of timelessness.

Several types of meditation techniques are used to induce OBEs. One involves the practitioner reaching a deeply relaxed state and imagining themselves floating gently upwards or drifting away from their body; binaural beats are often played during this meditation. Numerous examples of these can be found online and on YouTube.

Consistency is crucial for achieving out-of-body experiences (OBEs) through meditation. It's advisable to meditate daily for at least 15 to 20 minutes, ideally at the same time each day. This encourages your mind and body to establish a routine. Remember to let go of any fears or anxieties you may have, as they can hinder your ability to experience the process thoroughly. Keeping a journal to record your thoughts and experiences after each session can also be helpful. This allows you to monitor your progress and reflect on what you've learned.

One of the most debated topics about OBEs is whether they occur because of drugs or psychedelic substances. Many people report having these experiences after using certain substances, which can cause intense feelings and altered perceptions of reality. Some argue that these experiences are merely a result of the chemicals affecting the brain. Conversely, others believe they can lead to deeper insights about consciousness and existence.

Anyone who experienced the 1960s likely knows about the increased use of the psychedelic drug LSD. OBEs were often reported during this time, especially at major events like the Woodstock music festival, where thousands of people gathered. Many attendees claimed to have mystical experiences while under the influence of LSD or psilocybin mushrooms. The desire to explore consciousness and achieve a deeper spiritual awakening undoubtedly motivated their use, but, unlike spontaneous or meditative OBEs, using drugs to induce the experience can be addictive and is only as lasting as the drug's effects, often called a 'Trip' or 'Tripping.'

In 1964, Timothy Leary and a few others published a manual called "The Psychedelic Experience," which explained how to use LSD. This guide was based on the Tibetan Book of the Dead. It encouraged users to remain in a state of clarity, reminding them that this clarity was their true self. The message was to embrace the experience and not to fear the bright sensations, as they are part of who you are. This book became a popular resource for those exploring psychedelics during the 60s and 70s, especially at parties and festivals.

The use of psychedelic drugs to achieve spiritual awakening is a common reason for taking them, but not all trips result in this. Some reports describe bad trips. David took LSD at an outdoor music event with friends. He hoped for a mystical experience but began to panic when he saw his body floating below him; he was convinced he had died. Screaming, he ran into the crowd before collapsing and being taken to the hospital by emergency services. It was later revealed that he had a mental illness, which could explain his reaction.

A positive experience was that of James, a young man who attended a spiritual ceremony involving psilocybin. It was his first time at such a ceremony. At the end of the event, he described having an intense out-of-body experience in which he saw himself merging into something loving and not of this world. It left him feeling deeply grateful for life and led to a shift in his relationships with those around him.

David attended a common event; such ceremonies have been practised for centuries across different cultures. Usually, these ceremonies involve an experienced practitioner, like a shaman or spiritual guide, and are seen as chances for spiritual awakening.

Although these ceremonies are not legal in the UK, where psychedelics are used, they are often observed in many other countries. The more well-known include Ayahuasca ceremonies, where participants drink tea made from various leaves and herbs. The brew can cause vivid (OBEs), life reviews, and encounters with spiritual entities. Shamans conduct them and involve purging and spiritual cleansing; chanting often accompanies the ritual. The overall aim is said to be healing and establishing a connection with ancestors or spirit realms.

Psilocybin mushroom ceremonies are unique experiences designed to help individuals explore their minds and emotions in a profound and transformative way. These ceremonies differ from others because they can alter perceptions of time and space. Many participants report feeling as though they are floating or even having an out-of-body experience, where they sense they are outside their bodies. This can assist them in understanding thoughts and emotions that may be hidden in their everyday lives.

A key aspect of these ceremonies is chanting. Participants often sing or repeat specific phrases together, which helps foster a sense of connection and guides them through their journey during the ceremony. The sound of the chanting enriches the experience and can deepen their understanding of self-discovery.

Most often, these rituals occur at night. The darkness fosters a safe and tranquil environment, allowing individuals to focus inward without distractions. Combining the nighttime setting with the effects of the mushrooms and the rituals creates a potent space for personal growth and healing.

In summary, psilocybin mushroom ceremonies are more than simply consuming mushrooms. They include chanting, rituals, and the distinctive mind-altering effects of the mushrooms to assist participants on their journeys to self-discovery and emotional healing.

Peyote ceremonies involve using the peyote cactus, which contains the psychoactive compound mescaline. I will discuss mescaline in more detail later. The effects of mescaline can induce a euphoric sensation, which may include an out-of-body experience (OBE) or a sense of contact with spirits. Initiated elders lead these ceremonies and typically include dancing, singing, and spiritual storytelling. The purpose of these ceremonies is often regarded as a rite of passage, a means of trauma healing, and a pathway to identity transformation.

Ceremonies involving sacred plants or substances are not meant for casual use; they are seen as spiritual experiences that demand careful preparation and reflection. Participants usually need to fast beforehand and set clear intentions to engage with the ritual respectfully.

However, there are significant legal, medical, and ethical considerations to keep in mind. Legally, the status of these substances can vary depending on the location; therefore, participants must be aware of the laws in their specific area of residence. Medically, individuals should ensure they are mentally and emotionally prepared, as these experiences can lead to intense feelings and challenges.

Ethically, it is vital to respect the cultural traditions from which these practices originate. Participants should honour the heritage of the communities that have practised these rituals for generations.

Health-wise, individuals must be cautious about how substances may interact with any medications they are taking. Mixing certain substances can be dangerous, so it's essential to approach these experiences thoughtfully and, ideally, with the guidance of experienced facilitators.

In summary, although these ceremonies can be transformative, they demand thorough preparation, respect, and awareness of the different factors involved.

Reports of these experiences can be found in various media outlets, and numerous books have been written to describe them. In 'The Antipodes of the Mind,' published in 2002 by Benny Shanon, an account is given of an Ayahuasca ceremony attended by a middle-aged Israeli psychologist. He describes a moment when he felt as though he was outside of his body, observing himself lying on a mat in the Amazon jungle. During this experience, he underwent a vivid life review, during which he witnessed significant events from his life. He felt neither shame nor fear; instead, he sensed he was in the presence of divine intelligence. He remarked that he was no longer himself, yet at the same time, he felt more fully himself than he had ever been.

A report describing an experience from a psilocybin mushroom ceremony recounts the story of a young American man. A Mazatec healer supervised the ceremony. During the ritual, the man felt as if he was floating above the hut where the ceremony took place. He could see others singing below him and felt as if he had no physical body. When he returned to his body, he said he felt spiritually renewed.

Ceremonies connected to spiritual practices take place in various locations around the world. However, in the UK, some of these are banned by law. Nonetheless, other types of ceremonies that involve legal plants continue. Most of these gatherings are meditation retreats where participants practise breathing techniques. The main aims of these retreats are to attain spiritual awakening and, in some cases, to experience an OBE. Attendees often concentrate on relaxation and mindfulness, aiming to connect with their inner selves and gain deeper insights.

Perhaps one of the most well-known books inspired by the author's use of mescaline is 'The Doors of Perception' (1954), the work of Aldous Huxley. The book gained immense popularity during the 1950s and 60s and became highly influential. The rock band, The Doors, led by Jim Morrison, took their band name from the book.

In the foreword to the book, Huxley is depicted as a man driven by a desire to understand the mystery of human consciousness, a mystery that no one has yet solved.

Aldous Huxley volunteered to take a drug as part of a study conducted by Dr. Humphry Osmond, a British psychiatrist researching the use of psychedelics in his profession. The study took place in a private home, where a calm and safe environment was ensured, but it was also carried out scientifically, with detailed notes being taken. Huxley ingested four hundred milligrams of mescaline hydrochloride. Once the effects of the drug set in, he communicated his visions, thoughts, and feelings to Osmond, who was observing the experience.

Huxley described in detail the vivid changes he observed in everyday objects, such as flowers, drapes, and books. He noted that these items seemed to glow and took on much deeper symbolic meanings. This renewed appreciation for colour led him to experience a loss of ego and a sense of unity with the world; he felt no separation between himself and nature. Time appeared to slow down for him, allowing for a deeper way of seeing. He emphasised that this experience was not a hallucination.

Huxley believed that the brain usually filters out most of our reality to help us survive, but through mescaline, it opened the door for us to see more of it. He saw this experience as 'being pure' or the spiritual reality behind our everyday world. He firmly believed that this is how one should see things as they truly are. In other words,

Huxley was challenging our understanding of what is real and what is not. It raises the question: Does our ordinary consciousness enable us to see the complete picture of what the world is?

Besides spontaneous, meditative, and drug-induced out-of-body experiences (OBEs), some OBEs are triggered by trauma, acute pain, and other life-changing events. These experiences can happen in both children and adults and are often linked to trauma or Near-Death Experiences (NDEs). In children, certain situations, such as having a high fever or being in dangerous circumstances, can trigger these experiences. Children might describe sensations of floating outside their bodies, allowing them to observe what is happening around them from an elevated perspective. While these moments can be frightening or confusing, they may also bring feelings of peace or understanding.

It's essential to listen to and support children when they share these experiences, as it can help them process what happened and feel more secure. Recognising that such experiences can occur helps shed light on this fascinating aspect of human consciousness. The following examples of children's OBEs come from medical journals, personal stories, and studies about near-death experiences. These experiences can be very impactful and often leave a lasting impression on those who experience them.

Julie was taken to the hospital with a burst appendix. While under anaesthesia, she felt as if she were floating above her body. She was able to describe the medical team working on her, the instruments they used, and even the conversation they were having. Her account was later confirmed by the doctors, who found her observations to be accurate.

There are several stories about children who have experienced near-drowning incicents. In these situations, the children often describe struggling in the water. Interestingly, they report not feeling any pain or fear during the experience. Instead, many say they heard a voice in their heads or saw a bright light that reassured them, letting them know it wasn't their time to go yet. Afterwards, these children have been able to share the details of what happened with their parents, often revealing surprising accuracy about their experiences. It's fascinating and a little haunting to hear these accounts from such young ones, as they seem to have a unique perspective on life and death in those critical moments. It's common for the children to become less afraid of death afterwards.

In cases of terminal illness, children also report experiences of OBEs. Paula, aged 10, had an episode during chemotherapy and described floating upwards, seeing her mother crying, and the doctors panicking. She went on to describe a beautiful field and a feeling of being loved. Paula was calm, and although she did not understand the term OBE, she described its features. She declared that she was no longer afraid to die.

Seven-year-old James fell into a coma after contracting a viral infection. When he finally woke up, he described feeling as if he was flying above the hospital, watching other patients, nurses, and angels walk through walls. He reassured his parents, telling them not to worry because heaven was waiting for him. The idea of angels walking through walls isn't usually reported, but it might offer some comfort to his parents.

Out-of-body experiences (OBEs) often occur in individuals with terminal illnesses, and several common triggers have been identified that may contribute to these phenomena. Among these triggers are:

1. *Medication*: Certain medicines, especially those used for pain relief like opioids, can significantly affect a person's perception and consciousness. These substances may cause heightened sensations, a disconnection from the physical body, or altered states of awareness, making OBEs more probable.

2. *Pain and Distress*: The physical and emotional pain linked to terminal illnesses can cause intense discomfort. During moments of extreme distress, the mind may respond by dissociating from the body, resulting in an OBE as a coping mechanism to escape suffering.

3. *Near-death experiences (NDEs)*: People who have had NDEs often describe sensations of leaving their bodies, travelling through tunnels, or encountering bright lights. These powerful experiences can happen in critical moments. They might affect later episodes of OBEs, especially in those with terminal conditions.

4. *Fatigue*: Terminal illnesses often cause extreme fatigue and exhaustion. This overwhelming tiredness can lead to a state where the mind becomes more vulnerable to altered states of consciousness, facilitating OBEs as the body and mind reach a limit of physical and mental exhaustion.

5. *Fever and Infections*: Elevated body temperature from fever or serious infections can impair brain function. High fevers may cause delirium or altered mental states, potentially triggering OBEs as the brain processes intense sensory information differently.

Understanding out-of-body experiences offers valuable benefits. Research into OBEs is ongoing and essential to deepen our understanding of consciousness. The idea that consciousness might not solely depend on the mind is a compelling area for exploration. For those who experience OBEs, they are often regarded as therapeutic and transformative, providing crucial support in end-of-life situations. For others, they foster a new spiritual awareness and personal development.

A major difficulty in studying out-of-body experiences (OBEs) is their subjective nature, which makes it hard to verify them scientifically. Some people see OBEs as hallucinations, dreams, or illusions caused by neurological activity in the brain. Furthermore, others suggest that these experiences may arise from confusion and fear caused by trauma.

Whether you believe that OBEs transport us into another reality or are merely a mental experience, they remind us that our minds are full of mystery. We still have much to learn about our inner workings. What if the mind does hold secrets beyond our understanding? What if our consciousness does leave the body? Valid questions for us to consider.

8. Sixth Sense or Mystical Trickery

Perhaps the most controversial aspect of metaphysical experience is that of mystics and mediums. As far back as history can recall, there have been those who claim to be able to see beyond the veil, beyond what the human eye normally perceives. They are known by many names: mystics, psychics, fortune-tellers, tarot card readers, seers, prophets, shamans. The list is extensive. We encounter them everywhere, in fairgrounds, seaside resorts, churches, and across the internet, to name a few.

Many people claim to hear voices, see the dead, and predict the future, among other extraordinary abilities. Some have successful careers on television and are highly respected by those who seek their services. Others are mocked, but all seem to connect with us in some way and have done so throughout human history. Despite scientific advancements, rational beliefs in the supernatural persist. Tarot cards are found in bookshops, and newspapers carry horoscopes and columns by people like Mystic Meg.

So why do we still seek a reading and want to know what might lie ahead for us? It isn't that we are gullible, but rather, we long for guidance and to find some meaning in life. It's in our nature to be drawn by mystery. To have something more profound in our lives than mundane living. There is a clear shift towards spiritualism and enlightenment, particularly among younger generations.

Spiritual practitioners vary greatly, serving a wide range of 'spiritual seekers.' Some predict the future, others deliver divine messages, and some act as healers. All believe they possess extraordinary abilities. For instance, Mystics claim a union with the divine. Their practices involve inner experiences, often centred around deep meditation. They provide spiritual insights rather than future predictions.

Mediums differ in that they claim to communicate with the dead, serving as a link between the living and the departed. Many turn to mediums after losing someone close, hoping to receive a message. They do this through séances, automatic writing, and trance states. However, others, especially during stage shows, profess to sense the presence of spirits and often point out someone in the audience as the intended recipient of the message.

Tarot Card Readers use decks of cards which are adorned with spiritual symbolism. Depending on the order in which the cards are turned, they are said to offer insights into the person's life. One of the most well-known spreads is that of the Celtic Cross. The spread, which resembles a cross, uses ten cards, combining the present circumstances, challenges being faced, past influences and likely outcomes. The first six cards represent the centre or heart of the matter, while cards seven to ten show the external influences and outcomes.

Tarot card readers can be found across the internet, at fairgrounds, and seaside resorts. Some of the more well-known call themselves 'Clairvoyant to the Stars,' showcasing pictures of television and stage stars among their clients. One such reader was Eva Petulengro, who spent over fifty years in a small booth on Brighton's West Pier. She read palms and cards; her notable clients included The Beatles, Bob Monkhouse, and Michael Crawford, among others.

More outcome-focused than spiritually transformative are Fortune Tellers. Within that realm, we find the use of various tools such as tea leaf reading, crystal ball gazing (Scrying), palmistry, numerology, and astrology. In the case of Fortune telling, regardless of the tool used, it revolves around predicting events. Fortune tellers have existed for thousands of years across different cultures. They claim to foresee the future and reveal hidden truths and insights. Practitioners employ a mix of mysticism, psychology, performance, and, in some cases, genuine intuitive experiences. Perhaps one of the most renowned is Nostradamus, a 16th-century French apothecary and seer. He is said to have predicted the Great Fire of London, the rise of Napoleon, and Hitler. He did this using symbolic rhymes, which makes the accuracy of interpretation questionable.

I am very familiar with the legend of Mother Shipton and have visited her cave several times. According to folklore, she was born Ursula Southeil. She was an

English prophetess and fortune-teller who lived in the 16th century in the Yorkshire town of Knaresborough. Mother Shipton was said to have been born deformed, with a large, crooked nose and a hunchback. Like the features often linked to witches, she is regarded by many as a witch.

Ursula was regarded as a fortune-teller, prophetess, and herbalist, and was said to have made many predictions. Mother Shipton's prophecy book, which narrates her life and her more famous prophecies, was first published in 1641 and remains accessible today when visiting Mother Shipton's famous cave. The predictions she was known for included: the death of Cardinal Wolsey, the dissolution of the monasteries, and the Great Fire of London. Her grave is said to lie in unconsecrated ground on the outskirts of York and is marked with the following inscription:

Here lies she who never lied
Whose skill so often has been tried.
Her prophecies shall still survive
And ever keep her name alive.

Although many more areas of mysticism are practised, the world of the Psychic is one of the most notable. Within this realm reside clairvoyants who claim to see things invisible to others, those with clairaudience, the ability to hear voices or messages from unseen sources, and clairsentients who sense energies and emotions beyond their own. Mediums, who can communicate with the dead, possess telepathic abilities, and have a premonition of future events.

Whether psychic powers or enhanced ESP (extra-sensory perception) are real or fake is difficult to determine. Many supporters among the thousands of people who visit such practitioners report accurate readings, personal insights, and feelings of comfort during times of grief. They mention being told specific, personal information that could not have been known by chance. Genuine mediums and clairvoyants provide precise and accurate information rather than using generalised statements. Their accuracy remains consistent throughout the reading.

Sceptics, however, believe that most psychic phenomena can be explained by cold reading or hot reading, through confirmational body language or by using vague statements that could fit multiple situations.

Cold calling aims to establish a connection with the person or audience being addressed. It utilises a range of techniques that allow the reader to quickly gather extensive information by analysing the individual's body language, age, clothing, hairstyle, gender, sexual orientation, ethnicity, speech patterns, and level of education, among other factors. An experienced cold reader can be highly proficient in this field.

For example, consider a passage from a reading given to a woman who contacted a medium following the recent death of her mother. The session was recorded at the sitter's request. The venue was the medium's home, and the charge was £70 for a forty-minute session. The sitter was in her late 50s.

'I'm sensing a presence; it's someone from the spirit world. It's an older person who has passed away. Can you accept that?'

The sitter acknowledged acceptance.

'Oh, I am getting a crushing sensation in my chest, something to do with the lungs or the heart.'

'She had a heart attack,' confirms the sitter. Feeling the connection.

'She is telling me that you were very close to her and that you miss her greatly, but she is well now and happy. Her attack came on suddenly, and you weren't expecting it, but she says she was old and tired and had a good life. She is saying you need to move on with your life. She's laughing and telling me about the times you spent together. She says you were a challenge at times but always loving.'

It continues in this manner. By the end of the reading, no specifics had been provided. Nevertheless, the sitter was convinced and felt sure that the teller was in contact with her mother, and she questioned how else she would know about the heart attack. How could she tell if she was old and tired, or if it happened suddenly? You decide.

In cold readings, the sitter does all the work by confirming or denying what is being said. When the sitter denies, the cold reader will blame the spirit for unclear communication or leave it with the sitter. Often, a recap is used to reinforce validated information.

Many of the statements used in the example above are called 'Barnum–Style' statements, named after the well-known showman P.T. Barnum, renowned for his circus of human curiosities. They apply to stage shows as well as individual readings and there are generalisations that could fit many scenarios. One of Barnum's sayings, which he became quite famous for and often joked about, was that 'There is a sucker born every minute,' highlighting his belief that you can persuade people of anything if you tell them what they want to hear.

The statements used are those with which most of us can agree. A study conducted in 1949 by Bertram R. Forer, an American psychologist, is still referenced in psychology classes today. He gave his students what he claimed was a personality test. It included statements such as:

'You have a great need for other people to like and admire you.'

'You tend to be critical of yourself.'

'While you have weaknesses, you are generally able to compensate for them.'

'You have a strong need for other people to like and admire you.'

'You sometimes doubt whether you have made the right decision.'

Later, he provided them with a written report of the test's outcome. Most students claimed that the report accurately reflected their experiences. Forer had given them all the same report. His work, like the psychological tricks used by Barnum, clearly demonstrated that flattering generalisations, when explicitly aimed at someone, seem personalised and are likely to be believed, even when framed in broad statements that can apply to all.

The significance of Forer's work lies in highlighting how vague language in suggestions can influence our beliefs and expectations. This explains why many people find tarot card readings, horoscopes, and other psychic predictions to be surprisingly accurate. In essence, we want to believe them; they provide comfort and fulfil our desire to think that something exists beyond this world. We seek evidence that confirms our existing beliefs, which is why we focus on the reader's successes and overlook the misses.

At the opposite end of cold reading is hot reading, which has become increasingly easier with the rise of the internet. Hot reading involves the reader researching the sitter before the session. They might look up the sitter's surname, search for matching death notices, and access Facebook accounts with family information, including photographs. This allows the reader to describe the person's features accurately and provide details about their family.

Hot reading is, without a doubt, a form of deception. However, when employed on someone eager to believe in the medium's psychic abilities, it can be very effective. Methods such as booking tickets in advance, audience plants, hidden microphones, and common everyday eavesdropping among the audience while waiting for the show to start are simply some of the techniques used.

While hot reading might offer comfort and reassurance to some, it is also emotionally manipulative and exploits the grief and vulnerability of those it targets. It can be costly financially, give false hope of healing, and undermine those with genuine psychic abilities. Some mediums use both hot and cold reading, making it harder to tell whether a reading is genuine.

Over the years, many have tried to conduct experiments to determine whether a particular psychic, fortune teller, or mystic is genuine. Such experiments are usually carried out by scientists or sceptics aiming to disprove the existence of authentic psychic abilities. Some testing methods involve offering a substantial amount of money to anyone who succeeds in passing the test and demonstrating their abilities beyond doubt. To date, no one has convincingly shown, under controlled test conditions, that they possess psychic powers.

One such challenge was issued by James Randi, himself a stage magician. He was also a sceptic and often called out people who claimed to have supernatural powers. In 1964, he launched a million-dollar challenge for anyone who could demonstrate paranormal or supernatural abilities. Many attempts were made, but none succeeded. The challenge concluded in 2013. During an appearance on 'This Morning' (September 2011), Philip Schofield asked a well-known Welsh psychic to take the one-million-dollar challenge, telling her that the programme would cover all expenses to travel to the US to compete. She agreed. However, later she withdrew, calling the challenge suspicious and set up for failure.

It is worth noting that all tests conducted to prove or disprove supernatural powers are scientifically based and performed under controlled conditions. This does not account for the subjective nature of psychic gifts. For example, Edgar Cayce, an American who, at a young age, discovered he could enter deep, sleep-like trances, is often mentioned. During these trances, called the 'Sleeping Prophet', he is said to have given over 14000 readings, many of which related to health conditions, past lives, and reincarnation. Cayce died in 1945, but his numerous readings are recorded in several books. Although he did not author books himself, the only book published during his lifetime was a biography titled 'There is a River' (1942) by Thomas Sugrue. To this day, Cayce maintains a large following among people who believe in his gift.

The fact remains that the existence of psychic abilities is inconclusive, with no definitive evidence supporting or refuting their presence. What is certain is that stories of such powers have been passed down through generations, based on eyewitness accounts and personal experiences. Can we dismiss all such claims as fraudulent?

The problem with psychic occurrences is that they often happen unexpectedly and without warning, making them difficult to test scientifically. In moments of intense emotion or vivid intuition, individuals have reported psychic phenomena that feel very real to them but are hard to verify scientifically. Does that mean these experiences aren't real, or that some things will always lie beyond the reach of proof but not beyond the reach of human knowledge?

9. Ghosts and All Things Scary

In the late 1960s, in Castleford, Alice, a young single woman, moved into a flat above Pennington's Sporting Arms and Ammunition shop on Bridge Street. Happy in her new surroundings, she set about making it home. This is her story:

'It started innocently enough; the light would swing from side to side, and I would close the windows and check for drafts before jokingly telling them to stop. After that, I started to notice that things were not in the place I had left them, and the kitchen doors would be open as I was sure I had closed. Now I'm not the bravest of people, but strangely I felt no fear at the goings-on. I laughed at the idea of a ghost, but decided if there was one, I would call him Fred. As the months went by, I began to tell various people about Fred, and they all laughed at me. It didn't bother me; I knew something strange was happening, but Fred was clever; he never played to an audience. Then, my brother and his wife stayed overnight. Sue went to bed early and felt someone get into bed beside her. She thought it was my brother and

jumped up to find no one there. I had to calm her down and explain that Fred was harmless. While Fred didn't bother me, I was still pleased when a smaller flat came up and didn't hesitate to take it, wishing Fred good luck with the new residents.'

Alice, neither sceptic nor believer, consistently described the ghostly events she experienced. After she left, a family with young children moved in, and soon Fred's presence became evident. John, the new resident, takes up the story.

'I didn't believe in ghosts, but I do now. We had lights swinging and turning themselves on. The cupboard doors banged, and then the bed used to shake when we were in it. Then, one day, I was in the flat alone when I felt a hard slap on my backside. I spun around, but no one was there. I knew the wife and kids were out, but I really felt that slap. It was no figment of my imagination. I was scared.'

Phyllis, John's wife, continues:

'We used to laugh at rumours of the flat being haunted. Still, after experiencing the bed shaking repeatedly, I realised something was there. As the disturbances increased, I finally shouted at Fred to leave, making it clear he wasn't welcome.'

The activity reportedly ceased after the rebuttal. Research showed that an elderly man had previously lived in the flat and died there.

Fred's story may lack drama compared to others. He showed no malice towards Alice or the other family. Yet, two separate groups experienced similar events, raising questions about the reality of paranormal activity. All participants consistently recounted their experiences without exaggerating events or adding flourishes.

The truth is that few topics attract as much interest as ghosts. From traditional stories and TV adaptations to longstanding legends, personal experiences remain the most convincing. Our curiosity about death is reflected in our ongoing fascination with ghost stories. They feature in nearly every culture, influenced by local beliefs about death and what lies beyond.

But what is a ghost? Could it be the lingering energy of the dead? A spirit or soul trapped in time, or simply a trick of the mind caused by grief. As with many paranormal phenomena, we have not yet evolved to the point where we can measure or understand such events. We don't know what ghosts are, why so many people report seeing them, or whether they haunt places or individuals. Are they delivering messages from the grave? Some believe they offer hope to the living, proving that death is not the end. Whether you are a firm believer, agnostic, or a staunch sceptic, one thing is certain: ghost stories and sightings are here to stay, so perhaps, just perhaps, there is a reason they rise from the grave.

There are many types of mysterious phenomena, with ghosts often described as spirits of the dead trying to communicate with the living. Common signs include cold spots, moved objects, and unexplained voices. Ghosts are frequently linked to sites of trauma such as battlefields, hospitals, old houses, taverns, and historic buildings, usually seen along familiar pathways. For instance, some legends describe a Roman centurion walking the battlements or a grey lady haunting castle corridors.

Hans Holzer's Ghosts: True Encounters with the World Beyond (1963) gathers 150 cases supporting his view that ghosts are the spirits of the dead who remain on Earth due to trauma or unfinished business, implying that reality includes an 'other side.' Holzer claimed to have photographed ghostly figures, believed to be monks, while visiting Winchester Cathedral in 1964, using this as evidence that spirits often appear in historic sacred sites.

Holzer categorised three types of supernatural entities. These were viewed as residual energies or ghosts, spirits he regarded as intelligent and capable of interaction and communication with the living, and stay-behinds whose souls, for various reasons, remain earthbound. In all cases, he strongly believed that spirits can be sensed and photographed and that they deserve documentation and careful examination.

While most ghosts are seen as harmless, Poltergeists are regarded as more tangible and noisier. They are invisible to the human eye and lack a recognisable visual form. Occasionally, reports mention a shadowy figure or mist seen before poltergeist activity, mainly recognised for the disruption they cause, such as throwing objects, making banging sounds, knocking things over, and even causing injuries to the living.

Their presence is sometimes associated with intense emotional energy and trauma, often revolving around one individual with a haunting lasting from one to several months. As depicted in many films, the subject of the activity is typically a younger person, often female.

Colin Wilson, a British writer, philosopher, and researcher, has authored over 100 books on the occult and consciousness, including works on paranormal phenomena. One of his most renowned books is titled 'Poltergeist: A Study in Destructive Haunting' (1981). In it, he details one of his most famous cases, that of the Enfield Poltergeist, which occurred in North London between 1977 and 1979. The case involved a mother and her four children.

The mother reported banging, crashing furniture, levitation, and a mysterious voice sound. The case was examined by the Psychical Research Society, which concluded that the activity could be caused by unconscious energy. This supported Wilson's own belief that humans have hidden abilities that we do not use. He saw these hidden abilities as generating energy unconsciously, which could be responsible for poltergeist activity.

Reports of ghostly communication vary from audible voices and whispers to telepathic messages, dreams, and spiritual séances. Some individuals experience full conversations, while others sense emotions such as grief, fear, or longing transferred by apparitions.

Throughout history and across cultures, accounts of spirit interaction have involved practices such as automatic writing, the use of Ouija boards, and rituals performed by mediums or shamans to facilitate contact. These encounters often leave lasting impressions on witnesses, contributing to ongoing fascination and debate about the possibility of life after death and the nature of consciousness.

Poltergeists rarely speak, but they may imitate voices, knock in patterns, or produce screams and growls. Some argue that they are non-human entities, unconscious projections of the mind, rather than the spirits of the deceased.

Residual hauntings are often linked to old buildings, historic sites, and pubs or inns. They feature ghostly figures seemingly caught in a memory cycle, repeating the same actions repeatedly, such as walking through a particular wall, with footsteps heard at the exact spot and time of day.

Unlike residual hauntings, Interactive Spirits are believed to be spirits that wish to communicate with the living. They may be guardians, deceased relatives, or lost souls wanting to pass on a message or warning. It is said that they respond to questions during séances, which were popular during Victorian times.

Maybe the entities we fear more than poltergeists are what are called Demonic or Malevolent Entities. This type of entity is depicted during possessions in films such as The Shining and The Exorcism of Emily Rose. Their influence can be seen through marks on the victim's body, illness, fear, and intense phenomena surrounding the possessed individual.

The actual case of Anneliese Michel took place in Germany. Anneliese, a devout Catholic, began to experience seizures and was diagnosed with temporal lobe epilepsy. Still, despite medical treatment, her condition worsened. She then started to have terrifying visions, hearing voices and fearing religious symbols. Anneliese began to speak in different tones and languages she had no knowledge of, starved herself, and started to harm herself. It was claimed that several entities possessed her. Over 67 exorcisms were performed on her between 1975 and 76. She died in

1976 from malnutrition and dehydration. The Exorcism of Emily Rose is based on Anneliese's story.

So, what if there are any commonalities that exist across different cultures? The simple answer is yes. Nearly every society perceives spiritual entities as restless spirits, those burdened with unresolved feelings of grief, anger, and attachment. The witching hour, when most activity takes place, seems to be between 2:00 and 4:00 a.m. Most people share a similar range of experiences, including noises, sensing someone's presence, feeling emotional states, and seeing figures or misty shapes. Occasionally, multiple witnesses report the same activity.

Hauntings and other paranormal activity can affect children just as much as, or even more than, adults. In the case of children, it is said that their accounts are more vivid and detailed. This is viewed as being due to their imaginations and sensitivities, which many adults have lost in favour of reason and logic.

Jo, an eight-year-old, described seeing a woman dressed in unusual clothing who visited him and told him about living in the house where he now resided. He said that the lady would always keep him safe. Investigations revealed that an old woman had lived in the house.

As noted in the NDE section, many children and adults report seeing familiar ghosts, usually deceased relatives, on their deathbeds. These accounts often include vivid descriptions of encounters with loved ones who have passed away, sometimes offering comfort, guidance, or a sense of peace to those nearing the end of life. Researchers studying near-death experiences emphasise that such visions are shared across various cultures and age groups, though explanations vary. Some interpret these phenomena as meaningful spiritual events or evidence of an afterlife. In contrast, others suggest that they may result from physiological or psychological processes occurring in the brain during times of extreme stress or reduced oxygen levels. Regardless of interpretation, these reports continue to fascinate scientists and the public alike, prompting ongoing debate about their origins and significance.

During my research for this book, I received numerous accounts from people who had experienced ghost sightings, sensing the presence of something nearby when they were alone. Sometimes they would feel fear for no obvious reason. One event that stands out in my mind was described to me by a man who enjoyed walking and often strolled for miles through the woods and along tracks, unaware of the time or his surroundings. He explained that one day, while walking with a friend, they came across an old, abandoned orphanage they had known about since childhood.

They looked for a way in but only found a cracked board on a small window they couldn't squeeze through; every other door and window was locked and boarded up. The silence around the building felt disturbing. With no obvious entrance, they decided to head back home when suddenly they heard heavy footsteps coming from inside. He told me that the hair stood up on the back of his neck because it was impossible for anyone to be inside the building. They looked at each other, clearly frightened, when a loud bang, like a fist, struck the window nearby. Both started running but never forgot what they experienced. They never went back to the old building.

It resonated with me because I knew the old orphanage he mentioned and had often passed by it myself when it was filled with children's laughter. I also knew it had been abandoned for many years and was due for demolition.

One possible reason for the fear of the supernatural, particularly ghosts and apparitions, could be the numerous anecdotal accounts about such phenomena and our innate desire for safety. We know that one of our greatest fears is dying, ceasing to exist as we perceive now. Ghost stories suggest there might be something beyond death, but they are often depicted as frightening.

Fear of death is sometimes linked to its unknown aspects. Stories like that of the Grey Lady, said to haunt castles after a violent demise, mention mortality and the chance of tragic events. Many people encounter ghost stories in childhood or via the media, and these tales can greatly shape their perceptions. Consequently, when unexplained sounds, sensations, or sights occur, individuals may associate them with these stories, influencing how they respond.

At night, when you hear floorboards creaking or rattling windows, it's easy to mistake ordinary noises for something frightening. This reaction often arises from our current emotions, not merely a fear of ghosts or spirits.

The belief in ghosts goes back centuries and appears in folklore from around the world. Stories of spirits and apparitions have been used to explain the unknown and to pass down moral lessons or cautionary tales. During Halloween, not only do children wear costumes inspired by ghosts and other supernatural beings, but adults also take part in haunted house attractions, watch horror films, and decorate their homes with spooky motifs. Such practices strengthen the mystique and fascination surrounding ghosts. Overall, these customs reflect humanity's lasting curiosity about the afterlife and the supernatural, ensuring that the idea of ghosts remains a key part of modern celebrations and stories.

Is there any evidence for ghosts, poltergeists, or apparitions? Currently, no scientific proof has confirmed their existence, although many personal and cultural accounts describe experiences involving these phenomena. Such reports add to ongoing discussions about their reality, especially when numerous individuals report similar events.

Numerous investigations have been carried out into ghosts and the paranormal. The Society for Psychical Research, established in 1882, is one of the oldest and most respected organisations dedicated to examining paranormal phenomena through scientific methods. Based in London, The Society has published many books and journals, compiled of hundreds of cases where witnesses have claimed to see ghosts, and continues its work to this day.

The investigation explored hauntings, apparitions, poltergeist activity, mediumship, and telepathy. Although it uncovered many fraudulent claims, it remained receptive to the possibility that some unexplained phenomena might be authentic.

The Enfield Poltergeist is a case studied by two members of the Society for Psychical Research from 1977 to 1979. The events, which revolved around two sisters, Janet and Margaret, occurred in a terraced house in Enfield, North London. Witnesses, including police officers, neighbours, and journalists, reported seeing objects move, hearing unusual sounds, and witnessing alleged cases of levitation. The investigators, who stayed at or near the house, also documented reports of furniture shifting, knocking noises, and objects in motion, such as a curtain tied in a knot. Their findings suggested that about 2% of incidents might have been hoaxes by children, while they claimed that 98% could not be explained through conventional means.

Some observers questioned the reported activity, suggesting that Janet might have produced the voices using her false vocal cords; a speech expert observed that, while this is possible, it is uncommon. Psychologists offered alternative explanations, including sleep paralysis, hallucinations, manual manipulation of objects, or psychological phenomena such as teenage poltergeist syncrome, where young individuals under stress or trauma might inadvertently cause disturbances.

It was later claimed that the sisters admitted some fakery. At the same time, trickery could clearly explain some of the phenomena, but others could not be so easily explained, keeping the Enfield Poltergeist haunting a topic of controversy today. The activity reportedly stopped suddenly after eighteen months. Films, The Conjuring 2 and The Enfield Haunting, are based on the events that occurred.

Some researchers suggest that neurological, psychological, social, and environmental factors may contribute to reports of paranormal events. Although such experiences can seem genuine to those involved, these scientists offer naturalistic explanations for the phenomena. Ultimately, the question remains unresolved, potentially reflecting the complexity of the universe beyond current scientific understanding. Not all is as it seems!

We must acknowledge that, although hauntings are often recognised as fearful, some people report being comforted by such presences. They feel they are being watched over by loved ones who have passed away, even a form of communication that goes beyond the physical, a bond between the living and the deceased. We owe it to ourselves to remain open and curious about the unknown.

10. The Future of Psychic Phenomena

Nowadays, new technology is transforming how we perceive and understand the world around us. People often discuss how these changes could influence our perceptions of what happens after death or beyond our everyday experiences. In modern times, there is a clear divide: many depend on science to explain everything through facts and experiments, while others believe in strange or mysterious events that science has yet to explain. Although both seek to make sense of our reality, they operate with different assumptions, methods, and values.

We are now at a crossroads where new technology and innovative ideas about consciousness are transforming how we interpret strange or unexplained phenomena. This may lead us to find new ways to link scientific understanding with personal experiences that science cannot always explain.

For example, the aims of science are to explain experiences through observation and testing using empirically controlled experiments that can be repeated. Related to this is the belief that consciousness resides within the brain. In contrast, paranormal belief involves the investigation and validation of unexplained events through observation and the reporting of anecdotal experiences, and it recognises that consciousness might exist independently of the brain.

Perhaps it is the latter that causes such deep fear among scientists. If we proved that consciousness exists outside the brain, it could lead to a radical shift in how we view humanity itself. We would no longer be able to define a person solely by their biological brain, causing the boundaries between the self and our environment, mind over matter, to become much less clear. It would require us to rethink neuroscience and medicine, as we would have to consider the brain as a receiver or processor of consciousness.

The end of human life may mark the start of spiritual existence, offering new validation for NDEs, reincarnation, and ideas of collective consciousness. Considering this as a serious subject for scientific investigation is justified. The value of life and death would be understood more deeply. Quantum physics suggests that consciousness is universal, and there are signs of growing interest in connecting traditional science with the paranormal. Spirituality and consciousness become recognised as legitimate areas for open-minded scientific research, leading to a better understanding of human experience.

Why is it important to bridge the gap at all? Why not leave things as they are? The answer is simple: we need to expand human knowledge and understanding. As we have seen throughout this book, science alone is a long way from explaining all human experience. It is only by working together with open minds that we can explore the unanswered questions, particularly about consciousness and the reality of existence.

The experiences of individuals reporting paranormal events worldwide merit recognition rather than dismissal. Collaborative research could benefit areas such as palliative care, where healthcare professionals increasingly observe patients having spiritual or supernatural encounters. Such joint efforts may improve training for end-of-life care providers. Science does not possess all the answers yet, especially in understanding consciousness. Adopting a different research approach could yield valuable insights that may inform and challenge current scientific methods.

Increasingly, people are captivated by stories of the paranormal. Accounts of near-death experiences, mysterious lights in the sky, out-of-body encounters, and ghostly apparitions keep capturing our collective imagination. Every day, more individuals come forward to share their own extraordinary experiences, and it seems like everyone knows someone with an unbelievable story to tell.

At the same time, our bookshelves are filling up with new titles, some based on scientific research, others rooted in spiritual beliefs, all examining the many mysteries that science has yet to fully explain. Television programmes and documentaries on the paranormal are now regular fixtures in our living rooms, drawing curious viewers from all walks of life. Social media buzzes with discussions and debates, and communities dedicated to the unexplained are thriving like never before. With this surge in interest, a straightforward question naturally arises: Can millions of people sharing these stories all be mistaken, or is there something deeper that links these experiences?

Perhaps what attracts us isn't just the possibility that these phenomena are real, but also the hope that there is more to our existence than we currently understand. By keeping an open mind and listening to these accounts, we can broaden our perspective and even discover new ways to connect with each other and with the mysteries of life that make our journey endlessly fascinating.

If we look back through history, it's clear that many things once deemed impossible are now standard parts of our lives. Take space travel, for example: centuries ago, the idea of leaving our planet, let alone walking on the moon, was pure fantasy. Today, astronauts orbit Earth in space stations, and exploring the cosmos has become a reality. The same is true for flight. Before the

Wright Brothers' first powered flight in 1903, humans only dreamt of soaring through the skies. Now, flying across continents in a few hours is routine.

Technology continues to break down barriers previously thought impossible. Not so long ago, communicating instantly with someone on the other side of the world would have seemed like magic. However, today, we send messages, share videos, and have real-time conversations with anyone, anywhere, with just a tap on our phones. Advances in medical science have also changed our lives in ways our ancestors could never have imagined: organ transplants, treatments for diseases once deemed incurable, and prosthetic devices that restore mobility and independence.

Everywhere we look, the impossible of yesterday has become the everyday of today. This continually evolving story of human progress reminds us that today's mysteries and unexplained phenomena could be tomorrow's accepted knowledge. By staying curious and open to new ideas, we give ourselves the chance to explore the unknown and perhaps, one day, make the extraordinary ordinary once more.

Perhaps we're on the cusp between two worlds, one we know intimately and another just out of sight. Modern science has undoubtedly uncovered many of the universe's secrets, helping us understand nearly everything around us. Yet, let's be honest: many things remain beyond full scientific explanation. People continue to experience strange and mysterious events that don't fit neatly into scientific categories, yet they happen regularly. Instead of dismissing these stories, perhaps it's time we acknowledge that there might be more at play than we currently comprehend. Being open-minded doesn't mean discarding what we know; it simply involves being willing to explore the unknown. After all, every breakthrough begins with a question that had no answer, so who's to say that today's mysteries won't become tomorrow's facts? By staying curious and attentive, we may find new ways to perceive the world and ourselves.

11. Conclusion

Throughout this book, I have done my best to present both sides of the argument, those that emerge from scientific exploration and those from personal experience, spiritual belief, or the unexplained. I haven't claimed to have all the answers, but I have posed the questions that many people quietly carry but dare not ask. I haven't sought to prove or disprove anything, but I hope I have encouraged readers to keep an open mind.

In a world that often values only what can be seen, measured, or proved, many people feel lost when something extraordinary happens to them. How lonely must it be to have an experience that doesn't fit with anything you have ever known? Something you cannot explain but cannot dismiss either. Of course, not every unusual experience is a spiritual one. Our minds are very complicated, and our emotions and memories can play tricks on us, but metaphysical experiences remind us that reality may be more layered than we think.

You don't need a near-death experience or to witness something supernatural to feel that life is meaningful. Even if you haven't seen a ghost or had a mystical vision, you might still sense that love, connection, and wonder go beyond what we can see or explain. The purpose of this book isn't to persuade you of anything specific; it's simply to open the door to the idea that we are more than just our bodies, and that life could have a purpose greater than random chance.

As we move forward and continue searching for answers, I hope you'll view the world with fresh eyes and remain curious about what might be out there. Life is full of unanswered questions and mysteries that don't always fit the rules we know, but that doesn't make them any less real or significant. By staying open-minded and willing to listen to others and your own experiences, you might uncover a sense of magic in everyday life, and realise that the unknown isn't something to fear, but something to explore with hope and wonder.

Thank you for reading. Keep an open heart, ask brave questions, and let the mystery speak.

OTHER WORKS BY PATRICIA SUTCLIFFE

TORMENTED:

A riveting psychological thriller about a female serial killer tormented by the savage death or her mother and determined on revenge. Tormented surprises readers to the very end.

TALES OF OUR TIME:

Stories of the rejected. Their tales are harrowing. These are the unfortunates who have been left behind, abandoned, abused and discarded by society.

MEMOIRS/GHOST WRITTEN

Out of the Darkness
Hotel Tango 23
Handcuffed Emotions (best seller)
From Trauma to Triumph (best seller)
My Journey of Self-Belief

ABOUT THE AUTHOR

Patricia Sutcliffe is a retired university lecturer and a seasoned human behaviourist whose passions include both writing and chess. Her literary journey began early, at just ten years old, she garnered national attention by winning a prestigious school story writing competition. Since then, her creative output has flourished, with numerous poems and insightful articles on human development published in various outlets.

While Patricia delights in exploring an array of genres, her greatest dedication lies in uncovering and telling 'real life' stories. This commitment drew her naturally to the roles of Ghost Writer and memoirist, where she has found both professional success and personal fulfillment. For further information about her work, visit her website:

www.patriciasutcliffeauthor.com

If you have enjoyed reading my book, please leave me a review on Amazon. Your feedback matters to me.

Printed in Dunstable, United Kingdom